By Request 2

The Continuing Search for Hawai'i's Greatest Recipes

Also by Betty Shimabukuro

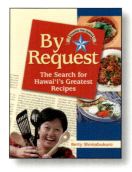

By Request:
The Search for Hawai'i's Greatest Recipes

By Betty Shimabukuro

Sought-after and hard-to-find recipes have been tracked down by *Honolulu Star-Bulletin*'s food writers and reproduced from their columns into this collection.

ISBN-10: 1-56647-773-5 • ISBN-13: 978-1-56647-773-4
Trim size: 6 x 9 in • Page count: 180 pp
Binding: Softcover, wire-o • Retail: $14.95

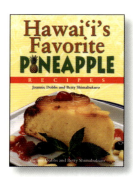

Hawai'i's Favorite Pineapple Recipes

By Betty Shimabukuro

Hawai'i's most popular and unique pineapple recipes along with vintage photos.

ISBN-10: 1-56647-566-X • ISBN-13: 978-1-56647-566-2
Trim size: 6 x 9 in • Page count: 160 pp
Binding: Softcover, wire-o • Retail: $13.95

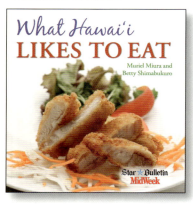

What Hawai'i Likes to Eat

By Muriel Miura & Betty Shimabukuro

What do Hawai'i folks like to eat? To answer this frequently asked question, two of Hawai'i's most knowledgeable followers of the local food scene researched fellow chefs, foodies, and experienced eaters. Here are their replies—over 130 recipes, including decadent desserts perfect for that sweet-tooth, favorites from the bygone days of fine-dining and friendly diners, Hawai'i Regional Cuisine, local plate lunches, and ethnic fare. All are easy to make. Some are familiar, some are new, and all of them we like to eat. Includes photographs of the food, chefs, and their restaurants.

ISBN-10: 1-56647-839-1 • ISBN-13: 978-1-56647-839-7 • Trim size: 9 x 9 in
Page count: 240 pp • Binding: Hardcover, wire-o • Retail: $31.95

To order these titles and more, visit
www.mutualpublishing.com

By Request 2

The Continuing Search for Hawai'i's Greatest Recipes

BETTY SHIMABUKURO

Mutual Publishing

Copyright © 2010 by Betty Shimabukuro

All rights reserved. No part of this book may be reproduced in any form or by any electronic or mechanical means, including information storage and retrieval devices or systems, without prior written permission from the publisher, except that brief passages may be quoted for reviews.

The recipes, stories, and photographs in this cookbook are reprinted with the permission of the *Honolulu Star-Advertiser*.

The information contained in this book is accurate and complete to the best of our knowledge. All recipes and recommendations are made without guarantees. The author and publisher disclaim all liabilities in connection with the use of the information contained within.

All brand names and product names used in this book are trademarks, registered trademarks, or tradenames of their respective holders. Mutual Publishing, LLC is not associated with any product or vendor in this book.

Library of Congress Cataloging-in-Publication Data

Shimabukuro, Betty.
  By request : the search for Hawaii's greatest recipes / Betty Shimabukuro.
     p. cm.
  Summary: "A cookbook of memorable, favorite, and popular recipes based on the Honolulu Star-Bulletin's By Request column by Betty Shimabukuro. This collection of local recipes include old favorites grandma used to make to unique dishes found at local restaurants"--Provided by publisher.
  Includes index.
  ISBN 1-56647-773-5 (pbk. : alk. paper)
  1. Hawaiian cookery. I. Title.
  TX724.5.H3.S54 2006
  641.59969--dc22
                              2006007020

All photos by Betty Shimabukuro unless otherwise credited.
The following photos © Star-Advertiser: pg. 17, 31, 48 (top), 59, 75, 123
   pg. 30 © Ayumi Nakanishi; pg. 48 (bottom), 64 © Ken Ige; pg. 31, 34-35, 78, 117 © Cindy Ellen Russell; pg. 82 © Jamm Aquino; pg. 8, 46, 94-95, 112, 118, 156, 170 © Craig T. Kojima; pg. 3, 55, 125, 147, 158 © George F. Lee; pg. 23 © Richard Walker; pg. 26, 38, 41, 61-62, 71, 105, 153 © Dennis Oda; pg. 27 © Kevin German; pg. 39 © Agustin Tabares; pg. 53, 87, 131 © F.L. Morris; pg. 77, 115 © Ken Sakamoto; pg. 80, 135 © Kathryn Bender
Photo on pg. 154 © Douglas Peebles
Spot photography from Dreamstime.com:
   pg. 56 © Tomboy2290, pg. 83 © Valentyn75, pg. 85 © Alexendregibo, pg. 106 © Danny Smythe, pg. 120 © Le Do, pg. 127 © Arnoud Weisser

ISBN-10: 1-56647-929-0
ISBN-13: 978-1-56647-929-5

Design by Courtney Young

First Printing, August 2010

Mutual Publishing, LLC
1215 Center Street, Suite 210
Honolulu, Hawai'i 96816
Ph: 808-732-1709 / Fax: 808-734-4094
email: info@mutualpublishing.com
www.mutualpublishing.com

Printed in Korea

Table of Contents

Introduction	vi
Dinner at My House	1
Sunnyside Up	16
Priming the Palate	31
Salads and Sides	54
Dips 'n' Dressings	69
Carbo Loading	86
The Main Event	99
Grand Finale	130
Recipe Index	162
Index	165
About the Author	170

Introduction

In all my years as a reporter, covering everything from breaking police news to mud wrestling, it wasn't until I started writing about food that someone responded to one of my articles by saying, "I think I love you."

Unfortunately, it was not Johnny Depp, but I appreciated the sentiment.

What did I do to deserve such a declaration? I found a recipe for someone who had been yearning for a dish she'd last had years ago at a restaurant that no longer existed. The taste was stuck in her mind; she wanted to make it herself.

This is the thing about food. For the most part, it passes between your lips and fills you up. At its most basic level it provides fuel and tastes decent in the process. At its best, though, it takes over a section in the brain bank, a place where flavor and memory fuse. It's not enough just to savor the moment, you want to recreate the dish and share it.

And this is what "By Request" is all about. The weekly column was part of the *Honolulu Star-Bulletin's* Food section for decades under the stewardship of several different writers, and continues in the new *Honolulu Star-Advertiser* under mine. Readers write in about dishes they've enjoyed at restaurants, that they remember from childhood, that they're just curious about. I try to find answers to a few of these mysteries.

This cookbook is a collection of stories and recipes that grew of out those requests. I can't claim the credit. "By Request" has always depended on the kindness of great cooks willing to share. Enjoy the tales, enjoy the recipes. And if you find something really good? Pass it on. Great dishes should always be shared.

Happy cooking.

Betty Shimabukuro
Managing editor
Honolulu Star-Advertiser

Dinner at My House

"By Request" takes a you-ask-I-tell approach. Recipe choices are driven by reader requests, which gives it an Everyman (or Everycook) appeal and leads to a much wider variety of recipes than if I made all the choices myself.

Still, the approach is self-limiting. If no one asks me for my favorite recipe for stir-fried beef with pickled mustard cabbage, well, it doesn't make the paper. And yet, it is a great dish and deserves to be shared with the world.

So I've chosen to begin this book with a collection of the dishes that I make for my family at home. Some are recipes that, like anyone else, I've clipped from the newspaper; others are part of our extended family tradition; a few I just stumbled across somewhere and they've became favorites.

If you were to come over for dinner at my house, I'd probably serve you something off this list.

Mustard cabbage—sin choy in Chinese—is a dark, slightly bitter green that's delicious when pickled.

This stir-fry dish is a sweet-sour mixture that's balanced just right to put all the best flavors forward. It's easy and quick. I'll often slice everything up and prepare the marinade in the morning, then have my son marinate the meat so that I can stir up the dish quickly after work.

Use less beef and more veggies if you like: crisp vegetables such as sliced celery, bell peppers and carrots work better than softer vegetables like zucchini or eggplant.

Pickled sin choy is sold in packages in Asian markets and Chinatown groceries.

Beef with Picked Mustard Cabbage
Serves 4

1 pound lean sliced beef
2 tablespoons vegetable oil
1-inch piece ginger, smashed and minced
1 small onion, sliced
2 cups (1 10-ounce package) sliced pickled mustard cabbage (sin choy)
2 tablespoons cornstarch dissolved in 2 tablespoons water

» Marinade:
2 tablespoons sugar
2 tablespoons soy sauce
2 tablespoons oyster sauce
2 tablespoons red wine or whisky
1 teaspoon sesame oil

Combine marinade ingredients and mix with beef. Let sit 30 minutes at room temperature.

Heat oil in skillet. Add ginger and stir-fry until fragrant. Remove beef from marinade, reserving ¼ cup marinade, and add beef to skillet. Add onions and stir-fry until beef is partly cooked. Add mustard cabbage with liquid from package, plus reserved marinade. Sitr-fry until beef is cooked. Thicken with cornstarch mixture.

Every Memorial Day, Dr. Jack Scaff, trainer of marathoners, opens his Round Top Drive Home to serious chili cooks, all competing for the championship in the Great Hawaiian Chili Cookoff. The winner of the top prize goes on to the International Chili Society's World Cookoff in Las Vegas.

The contestants are all serious pursuers of the art of chili, which means they don't use ground beef and they barely use beans. Their chili is chunky with beef, pork and sausage, slow-cooked with onions, peppers and specialized combinations of spices.

The 1999 winner was Jerry Hall of 'Ewa Beach, who called his concoction Jerry's Junkyard Chili. His recipe made 2 gallons.

It is my favorite chili recipe, although I've adapted it to make a smaller batch and I do add beans.

Junkyard Chili
Makes 12 large servings

1 1/2 pounds boneless cross-rib roast, in 1/2- to 1/4-inch pieces
1 pound boneless pork, in 1/2- to 1/4-inch pieces
2 medium onions, diced
1 tablespoon crushed garlic
2 tablespoons vegetable oil
1 15-ounce can chicken broth
1/2 cup chili powder (Gebhardt brand preferred)
1/4 cup cumin
2 15-ounce cans tomato sauce
1 large green bell pepper, diced
1 large red bell pepper, diced
1/2 pound Portuguese sausage, sliced
1 jalapeno pepper, minced
2 cans kidney beans

Brown meat, onions and garlic in oil. Stir in broth; cover and simmer 30 minutes.

Add remaining ingredients except beans and simmer 2 hours.

Stir in beans. Simmer until heated through.

Dinner at My House

ome things are magic and should be accepted as such without regard to logic or science. I propose we add cake mixes to that category.

Designed to be idiot-proof, your standard cake-out-of-a-box is made by adding eggs, vegetable oil and water to a pile of powder. Overmix, undermix, forget to grease the pan—you still get an edible cake.

But here's the thing: you don't even need the oil and eggs. Just get the batter wet—plain water will do—and you'll end up with a perfectly nice cake.

Learn something new every day.

Poke around the Internet and you'll find thousands of references to soda cakes: Sprite and white cake, Cherry Coke and spice cake ... on and on.

But why? Eliminate the $1/3$ cup oil and three eggs normally added to a box mix and you cut about 88 grams of fat and 600 milligrams of cholesterol. Plus it's cheaper, and you can throw a cake together even if you're out of eggs.

The formula: Add 12 ounces liquid to the mix, then follow the baking instructions on the box. That's a can of soda or $1^1/_2$ cups of any other liquid.

I made four cakes using Duncan Hines chocolate cake mixes. I tried Diet Coke, regular Coke, club soda and tap water, fully expecting the water cake to be a disaster. But all the cakes baked up the same, which would indicate that carbonation isn't the key. All four rose nicely, tasted chocolatey and were quite moist. The cola cakes had a slight husky cola flavor.

But why? A cake mix includes all the flavoring and sugar you need for taste, as well as powerful leaveners, emulsifiers and preservatives that make the cake rise, give it form and keep it from going stale. Apparently eggs and oil aren't crucial.

Wayne Iwaoka, a University of Hawai'i researcher who helps me with questions about food chemistry, says it is the gluten in the flour that supports the structure of the cake. The oil you add tenderizes the cake; the eggs support the gluten structure and also tenderize.

Iwaoka also said a cake baked without oil and eggs might dry out—the water would evaporate. This did happen with my cakes after a couple of days. The cakes were also so soft they were crumbly when cut.

A fifth control cake, which I made with eggs and oil, was much sturdier. If I were to do it over again, I'd add just one egg to the mix, for structure. I see no need for the added fat from the oil, though.

Actually, if I were to do it over again, I'd experiment with other liquids. Coffee, for instance, or whisky (whoo-hoo!) or even apple juice.

Cola Cake

1 box chocolate cake mix (any type, any brand)
1 12-ounce can cola (regular or diet)

» **Frosting:**
1 stick ($1/2$ cup) butter
$1/4$ cup unsweetened cocoa powder
$1/3$ cup cola
3 to 4 cups powdered sugar

Bake cake according to package directions, using cola in place of eggs and oil, in desired pan size. (If desired use 1 egg to make cake firmer.) Cool.

TO MAKE FROSTING: Melt butter over medium heat. Stir in cocoa and cola. When smooth, remove from heat; stir in sugar gradually to reach a texture and sweetness you like. Frost cake, or if cake is too soft to frost, squeeze a dab of frosting onto each piece, using a pastry bag or plastic bag with a hole cut in one corner.

A recipe is a terrible thing to waste. If your family's got a great one, or two, or a dozen, what's the point of keeping it trapped in the brain of one aunty?

Get it out there in the public domain, or at least the family domain. Use it or lose it, folks.

My mother-in-law turned eighty in 2006. To mark the occasion, her daughters and I thought we'd put together a cookbook of her best recipes—a keepsake to remember her birthday party.

My husband's mom, Beatrice Perez, hails from Guam, although she now lives in Las Vegas. She learned to cook primarily from her mother and carries most of her recipes in her head. She has five kids, fifteen grandchildren and a growing number of great-grands. It was these generations that decided the content of our little cookbook.

It was a noble plan, but easier said than done.

First came the process of retrieving the recipes from Grandma's brain. She'd produce a list of ingredients, then say, "You know what do." Well, no, not me. So we'd work up some instructions. And then her daughters, Nora and Lisa, would look over the results and the fine-tuning began: "Mom, you don't put sugar in your corn soup!" Or, "Mom, don't you put sour cream in the Tinaktak?"

And she'd say, "Well, it depends."

True mom recipes are that way: highly adaptable, based on what's in the pantry, or what's on sale, or how the tastebuds feel today.... Still, we got it all on paper and in the process I picked up some new techniques.

For example: browning sugar, a technique that Bea uses in desserts, but also with meats. Her Chicken Estufao recipe calls for browning chicken with sugar, which provides a coating for the chicken pieces as they begin cooking.

Chicken Estufao is a particular favorite of my husband, so the dish makes frequent appearances on our table. It's a Guamanian version of a vinegary dish that shows up in Portuguese and Filipino cooking, spelled a little differently: Estafao or Estofado. I started with Bea's recipe and have been working on it to make it my own. After all, I'm a mom, too. This has become one of *my* mom recipes.

Chicken Estufao

3 pounds boneless, skinless chicken thighs
2 tablespoons vegetable oil
2 tablespoons sugar
2 tablespoons cornstarch dissolved in 2 tablespoons water

» **Marinade:**
1 medium onion, sliced
3 cloves garlic, minced
³/₄ cup rice vinegar
3 tablespoons soy sauce
1 tablespoon fish sauce (patis)

Combine marinade ingredients. Pour over chicken pieces. Marinate 20 minutes.

Heat oil in pot. Add sugar and stir until sugar is light brown (be careful not to burn). Remove chicken from marinade (reserve marinade). Add chicken to pot, turning to coat with sugar.

Add reserved marinade. Simmer until chicken is cooked through. Taste and add water if sauce is too strong. Remove chicken.

Stir cornstarch mixture into sauce and simmer until slightly thickened. Pour over chicken. Serve with rice.

Dinner at My House

My husband has one cooking duty: barbecue. His specialty is chicken, Guam-style.

If you've never had the pleasure of attending a Guamanian fiesta, this is what you've been missing: chicken fresh off the grill with a lemony, slightly spicy, very smoky flavor that's nothing like local-style teriyaki or American-style barbecue.

Rob is the family expert at this dish. No one else even tries. (By the way, that's Rob Perez of the Goyu Perezes of Santa Rita, in case you're from Guam and think we might be related.)

Here is the recipe, with this caveat: your chicken probably won't taste exactly like his chicken, as the art is not in the recipe, but in the grilling, and that's hard to explain in writing. No matter. Unless you are a very lousy griller, your results should be good and chances are you've never had his chicken anyway, so what's to compare?

That's more or less what Rob told me as he poked holes in the underside of the chicken thighs before inserting them in his marinade. "I don't know if this does anything, but with barbecuing it's all in the ritual."

Moving on: you have to use a charcoal grill (well, it's not written in the law, but if you insist on gas, you're on your own). The heat must be kept high, so if you're barbecuing in batches, you'll need to add coals and stir them around. You'll also have to move the chicken pieces around, to take advantage of the hot spots on the grill and keep everything cooking evenly. You'll be creating a lot of smoke, so don't try this on the balcony of an apartment, and allow time for a shower afterward.

Also: use fresh lemons, but not fresh garlic. Rob always uses the pasty crushed garlic sold in jars. This bugs me, but you can't argue with success.

Barbecued Chicken
Serves 12

10 pounds chicken drumsticks and thighs, bone-in, with skin

» Marinade:
2 cups soy sauce
Juice of 4 lemons, about $^3/_4$ cup, plus 1 tablespoon lemon pulp
1 medium onion, sliced, about $1^1/_2$ cups
$1^1/_2$ teaspoons pepper
$1^1/_2$ tablespoons crushed garlic from jar
4 to 5 small red chili peppers

Combine marinade ingredients in large, nonreactive bowl, adding chili peppers last and crushing them while they're in the marinade. (If you happen to be drinking a beer at the time, add a little, for the ritual.)

Add thigh pieces, piercing the meaty side with a fork (don't pierce the skin side). Add pieces one by one, turning each one to coat and leaving it skin-side-down in marinade. Add drumsticks on top of thighs. Press down on meat so all pieces are submerged. Cover and refrigerate at least 6 hours, or overnight.

Prepare a hot charcoal grill.

Remove chicken from marinade and place on grill (if you're working in batches, grill thighs first). When coals begin to flame, cover grill. Grill chicken about 15 minutes on one side, removing cover when heat subsides enough that flare-ups cease.

Dip pieces in marinade and return to grill. Turn again after 15 minutes and check for doneness (cut into one piece). Continue grilling and turning chicken pieces, moving them around the grill so the most underdone pieces are in the hottest spots, until cooked through.

Dinner at My House　9

Once in a while a recipe will appear on my radar that is so intriguing I run out to the store to buy all the ingredients—prices be damned—and try it right away. This was the case when I came upon several online recipes for Crock-Pot Lasagna.

It looked too good to be true. You layer meat sauce, cheese and uncooked noodles in your slow cooker, then walk away for hours and come back to lasagna in a pot.

I am always looking for ways to make my slow cooker serve me better, but often the results are sort of vapid, a function partly of the vast amounts of liquid that accumulate as the food cooks.

Soups and soupy dishes such as corned beef and cabbage turn out well, but when it comes to stews and many other dishes, I prefer the results I get in the oven or on the stovetop, where you can count on the taste-boosting process of browning and the reduction of liquids into nice sauces.

But all that liquid you get in a slow cooker works to your advantage with lasagna. You need it to cook the pasta. If you did this in the oven you'd need to add a hefty pour of wine or other liquid.

The slow-cooker concept seemed both logical and magical. I studied several recipes, as well as critiques that said sometimes the noodles burned on the bottom or came out mushy. I made a few adjustments to cut fat and boost fiber, using ground turkey, nonfat cottage cheese, whole-wheat lasagna noodles and a layer of spinach and zucchini.

Everything went into the pot, and we went to the movies. Came home and there was dinner, cooked and ready. The noodles were tender, but with a bit of al dente chewiness, the sauce was flavorful, and the cheese was nice and gooey in that way that makes lasagna so comforting. The only thing missing was a browned top, but we didn't miss it.

Crock Pot Lasagna

Serves 8

- $1/2$ pound ground turkey
- $1/2$ pound (2 links) hot Italian sausage
- 1 cup chopped onion
- 2 cloves garlic, minced
- 1 29-ounce can tomato sauce
- 1 6-ounce can tomato paste
- 1 tablespoon fresh or 1 teaspoon dried oregano
- 1 tablespoon fresh or 1 teaspoon dried rosemary
- 1 pound non-fat cottage cheese
- 1 13-ounce box whole wheat lasagna noodles, uncooked
- 1 pound shredded mozzarella cheese
- 1 small zucchini, thinly sliced
- 1 10-ounce package frozen chopped spinach, thawed and squeezed of all liquid
- $1/2$ cup grated parmesan cheese

Lightly brown ground turkey, sausage, onion and garlic (don't cook until well-done or it will toughen in slow cooker). Add tomato sauce, tomato paste, oregano and rosemary. Stir well, heating just long enough to warm sauce.

Combine cottage cheese and mozzarella.

Grease inside of slow cooker. Spoon about 1 cup meat sauce onto the bottom of the slow cooker, covering bottom well.

Top with double layer of uncooked noodles (break to fit, using small pieces to fill gaps.

Top noodles with half the cheese mixture.

Add more sauce, another double layer of noodles and remaining cheese. Layer spinach and zucchini over top layer of cheese. Top with final layer of noodles. Pour remaining sauce over top. Sprinkle with Parmesan cheese. Cover and cook on low 4 hours or until noodles are tender.

Turn off pot and remove cover for a few minutes to let noodles set.

Dinner at My House   11

Fried rice is your basic use-up-the-leftovers dish. As long as you have rice, you can make it. Toss in bits of meat, vegetables, whatever's left over from dinner earlier in the week. This is handy, but means the taste quotient is better or worse depending on what you've mixed in.

A few years ago I started adding kim chee to my fried rice, no matter what else went into it. This turned out to be the glue that made it consistent in taste (and consistently tasty).

We eat this several times a month, and this is the dish I think my son would ask for if the world were ending tomorrow (well, along with pizza and SPAM™ musubi).

I still throw in whatever's in the fridge (and I always keep kim chee in there), but the oyster and chili sauces are basic. Everything else is flexible.

Spicy Kim Chee Fried Rice
Serves 4 as main dish

- 2 slices bacon, chopped
- 1 egg
- ½ cup chopped onion
- 2 cloves garlic, minced
- ½ cup diced bell pepper or corn kernels
- 1 cup diced cooked meat (chicken, ham, teriyaki beef, whatever you have left over)
- ½ cup chopped kim chee, or more to taste
- 4 to 5 cups leftover rice
- 2 tablespoons oyster sauce
- 1 tablespoon Thai chili-garlic sauce or kim chee base
- 2 stalks green onion, chopped

Fry bacon until cooked but not crisp. Push to side of pan. Beat egg and add to bacon fat in pan. Fold until mostly cooked. Push to side. Add onions and garlic to pan and stir-fry until softened. Add bell pepper and stir-fry a minute longer (if using corn, stir in later).

Push bacon and egg into center of pan and fold into vegetables. Add meat and kim chee (and corn, if using), folding until well-combined.

Add rice, breaking up any clumps (it's easiest to do this with your hands). Keep folding ingredients together until evenly mixed. Be sure to scrape pan and mix in any browned, crispy bits from bottom.

Combine oyster and chili sauces; add to pan and stir-fry until rice is coated and heated through. Sprinkle with green onions.

Making this dish requires faith. When you get all the ingredients mixed together it's going to look awful. Then you'll bake it for 30 minutes and it will still look awful.

But have faith. In another 30 minutes you will open the oven to lusciousness. Like magic.

Basically you mix a little uncooked macaroni and a lot of cheese in a pan, then add a sludge of milk and cottage cheese. In an hour the dry macaroni comes out all creamy and soft.

The original version came from the *New York Times* and ran in the *Star-Bulletin* in 2006. Within a few days, the requests started coming in for reprints from people who meant to save the recipe but forgot or couldn't find it, etc. This continued all year. I realized the appeal of this comfort food.

I bake this up several times a year—for my family, for potlucks, for fun. I have simplified the recipe and trimmed it down some with whole-wheat pasta and nonfat dairy products. It's still plenty sinful, though, the way mac and cheese is meant to be.

Magic Macaroni and Cheese
Serves 6

- $1/2$ **pound dry whole-wheat elbow macaroni**
- **1 pound extra-sharp shredded cheddar cheese**
- **1 cup nonfat cottage cheese**
- **2 cups skim milk**
- **1 tablespoon dry mustard**

Preheat oven to 375 degrees. Grease a 9-by-9-inch baking pan.

Combine macaroni and cheese in pan, reserving $1/4$ cup cheese.

Purée cottage cheese and milk in blender until smooth. Mix in mustard. Pour mixture over macaroni and cheese; stir until evenly mixed. Cover pan tightly with foil and bake 30 minutes,

Remove foil, stir well. Top with reserved cheese. Bake another 30 minutes uncovered, until cheese is set and macaroni is tender.

Let sit 15 minutes before serving.

Dinner at My House

The first time I made this salad, my son announced that the dressing was perfect for steak. So what if his culinary experience is limited to twelve years of living and eating? You know what you know and he knew this.

So this Lemongrass-Garlic Dressing has become my go-to dressing for salads topped with beef or chicken. It comes from chef Chai Chaowasaree's *The Island Bistro Cookbook* (Watermark Publishing, $32.50). The original recipe calls for New York Steak served over a salad mixture that includes shredded green mango and peanuts. Chai tells me he eats this almost every day, but since he doesn't like vegetables he just has the steak and the mango.

At our house we use a more economical cut of beef and mix of veggies. The dressing is the key here, and it will work with any vegetable combo your family enjoys.

Grilled Steak Salad

Serves 2

8 ounces tri-tip steak, grilled to medium-rare
¼ cup sliced onion
¼ cup sliced cucumber
1 cup bean sprouts
1 small tomato, in wedges
2 cups mixed greens

» **Lemongrass-Garlic Dressing:**
1½ tablespoons lime juice
1½ tablespoons fish sauce or soy sauce
1 garlic clove, chopped
½ tablespoon chopped lemongrass
½ tablespoon sugar, or to taste
½ tablespoon chili pepper, or to taste

Whisk together dressing ingredients. Taste and adjust seasonings.

Slice steak. Toss with dressing and onions.

Toss together cucumber, bean sprouts, tomatoes and greens. Just before serving, top with steak mixture and toss again.

You actually won't find this dish in a dinner at my house, but rather at my mom's. Betty Zane Shimabukuro (I was named for her; she was named for Betty Boop, a dubious distinction) is the master of many foods that are part of our family tradition. This one is her signature, though, the one that none of us has tried to duplicate.

Her note on this recipe says, "Dad's favorite, especially the head."

It is a classic Chinese-style preparation for whole fish that sounds simple enough, but depends on something extra, unexplainable—experience, technique, maybe TLC.

A key ingredient is one of my mother's secret weapons: chung choy, a salted preserved turnip that adds a burst of flavor in small amounts in many Chinese dishes. It is sold in strips that are rolled into a ball, in the Asian sections of most supermarkets.

How special is this dish? Sometimes my dad will tell my mom, "I was on the golf course thinking about your steamed fish." And then the two of then will go out together and shop for a fish.

If that's not love, what is?

Mom's Chinese-Syle Steamed Fish
Serves 2

1 pound whole mullet or kumu, cleaned
2 tablespoons peanut oil
Chopped cilantro, for garnish

» Marinade:
1 tablespoon soy sauce
1 piece chung choy, chopped, washed and soaked 5 minutes
1 tablespoon red wine
2 teaspoons cornstarch
1 teaspoon salt
2 teaspoons cooking oil
2 stalks green onion, mince
1-inch piece ginger, minced

Combine marinade ingredients and rub inside and outside fish. Stuff any remaining marinade inside fish. Put fish in a dish, a ti leaf or on a doubled piece of foil molded to fit fish, and place in steamer over simmering water. Steam 10 minutes.

Heat peanut oil until very hot and pour over fish to crisp skin. Garnish with cilantro.

Dinner at My House « 15

Sunnyside Up

Breakfast can be as simple as toast and coffee, but to really jump start your day you want something with more substance and flavor. Unfortunately, the first meal of the day tends to get the least attention. Mornings are so rushed, it's often impossible to work in the time to bake.

Sometimes, though, a little planning the day before can mean a tasty, hot breakfast in the morning. The aroma will certainly get the family moving. Then again, there's always the weekend.

March 3, 2004

Got bananas? Are they nice and mushy? Today's topic is baking with bananas, featuring a banana and poi quick bread from Kaka'ako Kitchen, provided here by creator Lisa Siu.

Of course, everyone's got a favorite banana bread recipe, so for one to stand out, it's got to have a something extra. In Siu's recipe, it's poi. Her loaf contains 1/4 cup of poi, but if you have some irrational fear of the pasty gray stuff, don't worry: this bread will not turn out all health-foody and strange. It also includes butter, sugar, eggs and sour cream.

Taro, the sole ingredient (save water) in poi, has a few advantages when it comes to baking. At the University of Hawai'i's College of Tropical Agriculture and Human Resources, research has been conducted on how, exactly, this works. A food scientist there once told me that taro works well in combination with baked goods because it is high in a substance called soluble gum, which provides a "mouthfeel" of thickness and richness, even though taro is fat-free.

This property of taro is unique among starches. Potatoes don't have it. Oatmeal is close, but because of its high fiber content, it produces a grainier baked good, whereas using poi gives you a smooth, soft bread (imagine taro rolls).

This all gives the Kaka'ako poi bread its advantage.

Kaka'ako Kitchen Banana-Poi Bread

1/2 cup butter
1 1/4 cup sugar
1/4 cup poi
2 teaspoons vanilla
2 eggs
1/4 cup sour cream
1 cup mashed overripe bananas
1 1/2 cups flour (all-purpose or bread flour)
1 teaspoon baking soda
1/2 teaspoon salt

Preheat oven to 350 degrees.

Cream butter, sugar, poi and vanilla until fluffy. Add eggs one at a time, then mix in sour cream and bananas.

Combine flour, baking soda and salt. Add to wet ingredients and stir to combine. Do not overmix. Pour batter into an ungreased 9-by-5-inch loaf pan. Bake 45 to 55 minutes.

January 28, 2009

Once upon a time, the old Garden Court restaurant at Liberty House in Ala Moana Center was the ideal place for ladies who lunched. Or brunched.

I've received frequent requests—usually from ladies—for the Garden Court's biscuits, which I never had the pleasure of consuming, but which seem to have legions of devoted fans.

My baking buddy, Susy Kawamoto, a devoted recipe collector and frequent solver of "By Request" mysteries, found this recipe in her files. She says she cut it out of a newspaper long ago.

This recipe calls for a lot of baking powder (3 tablespoons—that's not a mistake), for lightness. The original made a LOT of biscuits, so I've reduced it by a quarter, as well as expanded on the instructions a bit for home use.

Biscuits are a simple baking project, but I suspect the cooks at the Garden Court mastered their technique so that the end result was out of the ordinary. The trick would be in handling the dough gently to keep the biscuits light.

The original recipe did not specify what kind of baking pan to use. I opted for a round cake pan, which gives you wedge-shaped biscuits. You could also cut them into individual round biscuits.

One final note: By happy accident, when I made my first batch, I accidentally put in too much sugar—1/4 cup instead of 2 tablespoons (I was dividing the recipe in my head and math is always a dicey thing with me). But I actually liked this sweeter version better.

If you plan to serve your biscuits with honey or jam, maybe you don't need the extra sweetness, but I offer the suggestion for those who'd like to experiment.

Liberty House Garden Court Biscuits

2 cups flour
2 tablespoons sugar
3 tablespoons baking powder
1/2 teaspoon salt
1/4 cup plus 3 tablespoons softened butter
1 egg
1/2 cup milk
1 egg, slightly beaten with 1 teaspoon water

Preheat oven to 375 degrees. Butter a 9-inch round baking pan.

Combine flour, sugar, baking powder and salt. Cut in butter until mixture resembles coarse sand.

Beat egg and milk together and add to flour mixture. Mix gently to moisten all ingredients. Do not overmix. If batter is dry, add a little more milk.

Form dough into ball and turn onto lightly floured surface. Knead lightly while forming dough into a circle.

Roll with a rolling pin until about 3/4-inch thick. Sprinkle with flour if necessary to prevent sticking. Place dough in prepared pan and score through with a floured knife to form 8 wedges. Brush top with egg/water mixture.

Bake about 20 minutes, until golden on top and cooked through in the center. Break biscuits apart and serve hot or warm.

February 17, 2010

Bread pudding is a classic way to use up leftovers. Of course, keeping the bread from going to waste requires an additional investment in eggs and cream, but then you get to eat a nice, warm slice of bread pudding. Probably worth it.

Celeste Mendiola-Flores, pastry chef for the country club, says she makes 10 pans of this bread pudding each week—and these are what they call "hotel pans," 12 by 20 inches. The treat is served on buffets and is often requested for private functions.

Now, you can find 12-by-20-inch disposable aluminum roasting pans if you want to make the full recipe. But keep in mind that you have to set up a water bath, which means that the big pan has to fit inside an even bigger pan filled with hot water. This combo will not fit in a standard oven. And besides, how many people are you serving?

For practical purposes, I've cut the recipe in half. Use a half-size pan, 10 by 12 inches and $2\frac{1}{2}$ to 3 inches deep. These are also easy to find in supermarkets. Get one of the full-size pans, too, for your water bath.

Mendiola-Flores uses dinner rolls, which she slices "to give it that nice, thin-sliced appearance and texture." But she emphasizes that this is just her preference. Tear the bread if you like or if you've got only scraps. "There is no right or wrong way."

And she offers a tip: It's easier to slice bread when it's frozen.

Oahu Country Club Bread Pudding

Serves 12

1¼ pounds dinner rolls (preferred) or day-old white bread
¼ cup raisins, optional
9 large eggs
2¼ cups sugar
¼ teaspoon salt
¾ tablespoon vanilla extract
7 cups whole milk
2 cups heavy cream

Preheat oven to 350 degrees. Spray a 10-by-12-inch aluminum pan with cooking oil spray.

Slice dinner rolls or break bread into pieces. Place in pan. Sprinkle with raisins, if using, and set aside.

Beat eggs and add sugar, salt and vanilla; whisk until fluffy. Add milk and cream; mix well, then strain (this mixture is called guss). Pour evenly over bread in pan. Make sure bread absorbs most of the guss.

Spray sheet of foil with cooking oil spray. Cover pan loosely with foil. Place pan into larger pan to create water bath. Place pans in oven. Add warm water to outer pan, about halfway up the sides. Bake 90 minutes.

Check pudding for doneness. Top should be firm, but center might be a little jiggly. It will set as it cools. Serve warm.

Sunnyside Up

May 7, 2008

As Mother's Day approaches (it's Sunday, in case you forgot), some advice from a mom: "You have to learn how to cook or your husband will leave you."

OK, so it's advice that's frozen in time, space and attitude, but it sunk in with Rosario Tarvyd. "My sisters and I are very domesticated," she says.

They all learned to cook from their mother in the Philippines; then Rosario married an American, Chris Tarvyd, and moved to Hawai'i. And she cooks, but then, so does he. In fact, they're cooking together in the semiprofessional ranks, in a traveling show called Crepes No Ka 'Oi. On weekends, they load up a truck with propane-fueled crêpe makers and other supplies and head for a fair or festival to dish up crêpes-to-go.

Crêpes are a good idea for Mother's Day—a bit more complicated than pancakes, which shows you've put some effort into the matter. Plus they're pretty, befitting a holiday. And they can be served as breakfast for early-rising moms, or made into a savory lunch dish for those who are sleeping in.

"A crêpe is very versatile, so anything you want to put in it—chicken, beef, spinach, mushrooms, onions—those are all possibilities," Rosario says.

Peanut butter's great, she says, with chocolate syrup squeezed out of a plastic bottle. Not to mention simple fruit preserves straight from the jar. Folded into a golden crepe and topped with whipped cream—you've got a special-event dish.

Their best advice is to use a good nonstick skillet, or well-seasoned cast-iron skillet. The only tricky part is learning to turn the crêpe, but once you've mastered that, the project is simple enough for kids.

If your aim is a Mother's Day surprise and you've never done this before, a little practice before Sunday may be in order. Crêpes can be made ahead, stacked between waxed paper and frozen—or you can save extra batter in the refrigerator so you can cook them up fresh. Give the batter a good stir and let it sit out to take the chill off before cooking.

The Tarvyds warn that the first crêpe of every batch is usually a throwaway. It tears or doesn't cook evenly. This happens even to the pros. So don't be discouraged. Move on.

» Sunnyside Up

Crêpes
Makes about 12 crepes

» **Crepe Batter:**
  1 cup flour
  Pinch salt
  1 egg
  1 egg yolk
  1½ cups whole milk
  1 tablespoon unsalted butter, melted and cooled
  ½ teaspoon vanilla
  Filling of your choice (see below)

Sift flour and salt into mixing bowl. Create a well in center and add eggs. Slowly add half the milk, stirring constantly. Add butter and vanilla. Beat until smooth, while adding remaining milk. Cover and let sit 20 minutes or more.

Spray 10- to 12-inch nonstick skillet with cooking spray and place over medium-high heat. Pour ¼ cup batter into skillet and tip from side to side until batter covers bottom of pan. Turn when bottom is golden brown. Transfer to plate.

Spread with filling. Fold. Serve warm.

» **Easy fillings, mix and match:**
  Sliced fruit, such as bananas or strawberries
  Peanut butter, with or without jelly
  Chocolate syrup
  Nutella (hazelnut spread)
  Fruit preserves, such as strawberry jam
  Canned pie fillings
  Shredded cheese
  Leftover rotisserie chicken
  Diced ham
  Butter and sugar

Sunnyside Up

May 6, 2009

"**I** am enclosing an address label, a stamp, and a hope."

So wrote Su Conahan in a letter outlining her search for a bread she used to buy at a Japanese supermarket in Sacramento, California, made by a baker in Seattle "who has long since disappeared from the phone book."

It was called Malia's Old-Style Portuguese Milk Bread. Conahan even enclosed a copy of the label, listing ingredients that included potatoes, milk, eggs, flour, etc. It seems she's been combing cookbooks for a long time but can't find the right combination of ingredients.

I can't guarantee this recipe will match Malia's—it doesn't have eggs, for one thing—but it's a really good loaf of bread. You could easily tinker with it by experimenting with a few substitutions or by baking a round loaf instead of using a loaf pan.

Pão de Leite, or milk bread, is made with a scoop of mashed potatoes, along with milk and a bit of the potato cooking water. It's not the same as Portuguese sweet bread. This is a good, all-purpose white bread—soft and very easy to slice. Spread it with butter and your favorite jam, or use it for sandwiches or to accompany soups, stews or chili.

This recipe is adapted from *Flavors of Aloha: Hawai'i's Ethnic Foods*, published in 2001 by the Japanese Women's Society of Hawai'i. It can easily be doubled.

A note to beginning bread-makers: After you add the yeast to the warm water and sugar ("proofing"), the mixture should become foamy. If you get no reaction, your yeast could be dead, or the water might have been too cool to activate the yeast, or too hot, in which case you killed the yeast. Start this portion of the recipe over.

Portuguese Milk Bread (Pao de Leite)

Makes 2 loaves, about 10 slices each

1 medium potato
1$^1/_2$ cups whole milk
$^3/_4$ cup vegetable shortening
1 package (2$^1/_4$ teaspoons) active dry yeast
$^1/_2$ cup sugar
5 cups flour
$^1/_2$ tablespoon salt

Peel potato and cut in large chunks. Boil in pot of water until very soft. Reserve $^1/_4$ cup of water from pot; drain the rest. Mash potatoes to make $^1/_2$ cup. Let reserved potato water cool to 100 to 110 degrees.

Meanwhile, scald milk (heat to just below boiling). Remove from heat and stir in shortening to melt. Let cool to lukewarm.

Place warm potato water, yeast and 2 tablespoons sugar in large mixing bowl. Stir, then let sit a few minutes until foamy. Add mashed potatoes to yeast mixture.

Combine 4 cups flour with salt and remaining sugar. Add 1 cup of this mixture to yeast mixture, beating well with mixer or with the bread hook of a standing mixer. Add milk mixture, alternating with flour mixture to make a stiff dough (ending with flour mixture).

Place dough on lightly floured board. Knead in remaining cup of flour, gradually, until dough is smooth and elastic, 5 to 8 minutes (if needed, use up $^1/_2$ to cup more flour). Place in a greased bowl, turning to grease dough on all sides. Cover and let rise until doubled, about 2 hours.

Grease 2 5-by-9-inch loaf pans. Divide dough in half. Shape each half into a loaf and place loaves in pans. Cover, let rise again until doubled, 1 hour to 90 minutes.

Preheat oven to 325 degrees. Bake 45 minutes, or until light brown and cooked through.

Sunnyside Up « 25

November 12, 2008

Oatmeal cakes have been on the menu at Big City Diner since the restaurant opened. Senior Executive Chef Dennis Franks said they were created to offer diners something better for them than eggs and bacon, but more interesting than a traditional bowl of oatmeal.

The ingredients—oatmeal, sugar, water and raisins—are cooked up just like your regular Quaker Oats, but it's a much thicker mix. So thick that when patted into a pan, it firms up into a "cake" dense enough to slice. Wedges are then browned on the griddle.

At Big City Diner, this cake is prepared in an 18-by-12-inch commercial baking pan. The best alternative for home baking would be a standard cake pan. I've reduced the original recipe to fit.

You'll notice that the cakes are almost fat-free, but they do include a lot of brown sugar. I've given samples to a few people who say they were too sweet. If you prefer, you could easily cut back on the sugar or use a sugar substitute.

Big City Diner Oatmeal Cakes
Serves 6

- 8 cups water
- 1½ teaspoons salt
- 2 tablespoons cinnamon
- 1 cup brown sugar, packed
- ½ heaping cup raisins
- 6 cups quick-cooking oatmeal
- 1 tablespoon butter

Combine water and salt, cinnamon and sugar in large pot. Bring to boil.

Add raisins and oatmeal. Cook over medium heat, stirring frequently, until very thick, 3 to 5 minutes. Spread evenly in a 13-by-9-inch pan and let cool.

Cut into 6 squares, then cut each square in half diagonally to form 12 wedges.

Melt butter in skillet and brown each wedge lightly on all sides, including cut edges (to keep oatcake nearly fat free, use a cooking oil spray instead of butter). Serve with honey and fresh fruit.

July 25, 2007

Paul Chun, president and chief executive officer of Chun Kim Chow Ltd., died June 21 at age eighty-four. His company had extensive real estate and retail holdings, including the Robins shoe stores and the Waikīkī Circle Hotel. But his hobby was cooking. "Every Sunday was an extravagant nine-course meal," his daughter, Pamela Chun-Ganske, says.

During the West Coast dock strike in 1971, the hotel ran out of pancake mix, so Chun put his skills to work and developed a scratch pancake recipe by studying cookbooks in bookstores (he didn't actually buy one, his daughter says).

The recipe became the hotel restaurant's signature; people would line up for the 99¢ plate of two pancakes, eggs and breakfast meat. At his funeral, the family passed out the recipe. A nice way to remember someone, isn't it?

His daughter says she still makes them every Sunday. "I tear up every time."

I gave the recipe a test run, and at first thought something was wrong: there was so much baking powder that the batter got all frothy. But this turns out to be the secret to a light, fluffy pancake. I've modified the formula slightly to expand on the instructions.

Paul Chun's Pancakes
Makes about 12 pancakes

2 cups flour
3 tablespoons baking powder
Dash of salt
3 or 4 tablespoons sugar
3 eggs, separated
1¼ cup milk
⅓ block melted butter, cooled

Combine dry ingredients. Beat yolks slightly and add, along with a little milk. Stir.

Beat egg whites and add, along with a little more milk. Add melted butter. Stir and gradually add enough of the remaining milk so batter is of the right consistency (this is a judgment call—it shouldn't be too thin and should still have lumps, but needs to be loose enough to scoop easily). Batter will get very fluffy as baking soda activates; do not be alarmed. Do not overmix. Let sit 10 to 15 minutes to settle.

Preheat griddle or skillet over medium heat. Pour about ¼ cup batter for each pancake. Turn when edges are dry and bottom is golden.

March 19, 2008

Jean Sumimoto was three months old when her father, George Abe, opened a bakery in the back of the Piggly Wiggly store on Oneawa Street in Kailua. The proud papa named the bakery for his baby, calling it Jean's Bakery & Fountain.

This was in 1950; the bakery remained open until 1972, although Abe eventually moved it to a freestanding location on Ulunui Street. As the oldest of the four Abe kids, Sumimoto put in her time at the bakery, working on such specialties as the marzipan bunnies and bunny cakes made at Easter. "From fifth grade I was selling doughnuts," Sumimoto says.

Abe is ninety-two and remains active with tennis and bowling, but he's left the baking behind. The one recipe that survives from the old bakery is his Danish Tea Cake, a buttermilk cake topped with a maple-flavored glaze and chopped nuts. The cake was a favorite of Sumimoto's Aunty Alice, so it's the one recipe that's been preserved.

Abe scaled it down from the large commercial quantity and Sumimoto further refined it. She tested it several times before sharing it here.

Note that Sumimoto and her dad measured out their ingredients by weight, which is the best way to get exact results. For those without scales, though, volume measurements are included here.

28   Sunnyside Up

Jean's Bakery Danish Tea Cake

12 ounces (1^3/$_4$ cups, unpacked) brown sugar
6 ounces (^{3}/$_4$ cup) white sugar
1^1/$_4$ teaspoon salt
1 teaspoon vanilla
6 ounces (^{3}/$_4$ cup) vegetable oil
12 ounces (1^1/$_2$ cups) buttermilk, divided use
11 ounces (2^3/$_4$ cups) cake flour
1 tablespoon baking powder
1^1/$_2$ teaspoons baking soda
3 large eggs
^{1}/$_2$ cup chopped macadamia nuts

» **Glaze:**
^{2}/$_3$ cup powdered sugar
1 tablespoon water
2 to 3 teaspoons maple syrup

Preheat oven to 350 degrees. Grease and flour 2 8-inch round cake pans.

Combine sugars, salt and vanilla. Mix in oil and ^{1}/$_2$ the buttermilk.

Sift together flour, baking powder and baking soda. Add to sugar mixture. Add remaining buttermilk and eggs. Mix well (batter will be very thin). Pour into prepared pans. Bake about 40 minutes.

Cool cake, then drizzle with icing and sprinkle with chopped nuts.

Sunnyside Up   29

July 9, 2008

Why don't we bake more pineapple bread? Given our history with the fruit, you'd think local cookbooks would be full of recipes—but, no.

Banana and mango breads are our quick breads of choice, but pineapple really deserves a shot. For one thing, it's extremely simple. Buy a can of crushed pine, open it and dump it in the mixing bowl. It's quicker even than peeling and mashing a banana, and definitely easier than peeling and slicing a mango.

The great thing about quick breads is that most recipes are very forgiving. If you don't have the size of pan called for in the recipe, using a size bigger or smaller is usually OK. If you don't like nuts, leave them out. If you want a stronger pineapple flavor, add more, cut in chunks.

Pineapple Nut Bread

1¾ cups flour
2 teaspoons baking powder
½ teaspoon salt
¼ teaspoon baking soda
¾ cup chopped macadamia or walnuts
¾ cup packed brown sugar
3 tablespoons butter, softened
2 eggs
1 cup crushed pineapple, undrained
2 tablespoons sugar
½ teaspoon cinnamon

Preheat oven to 350 degrees. Grease 9-by-6-inch loaf pan. Sift together dry ingredients. Stir in nuts.

Cream brown sugar, butter and eggs. Stir in dry ingredients (mixture will be dry); fold in pineapple. Pour into loaf pan.

Combine sugar and cinnamon; sprinkle over loaf. Bake 50 to 60 minutes.

Priming the Palate

They're called appetizers for good reason. They prime the tastebuds and get the brain set for the main event.

And another thing: Appetizers encourage sharing. While an entrée is divided among individual plates, the pūpū platter is placed at the center of the table so everyone can have a taste—a scoop of dip, a couple of shrimp, a wedge of quesadilla.

Round up enough of them and who even needs a main dish?

March 11, 2009

Lucky you live Hawai'i, yeah? For the best in mangoes, lychee, laulau. Not to mention easy access to SPAM™ musubi. And butter rolls.

I never figured butter rolls for an only-in-Hawai'i thing. It's not as though yeast and white flour are grown here. But enough people have reported to me that when they moved away they could no longer find those soft buns ... and so I accept this as truth.

One of my mainland readers did the best job of explaining the difference: She yearns for a light, buttery roll with a "hat" on top, as though the roll were baked in a muffin tin. You know: it looks like a giant mushroom, and apparently our brethren on the mainland just don't make 'em that way.

Well, calls to a few local bakeries didn't help. At one, they told me their dough comes to them frozen from New Zealand (!) and they just bake the buns up here. So much for the local-exclusivity theory.

But anyway, the clue I got there was the name that bakery uses for the buns: Butterflake Rolls.

A search of a number of baking cookbooks turned up zilch, or rather, many recipes with the right name and the wrong approach, but I finally found one that called for a muffin tin. I tried it a couple times, tasted it against those frozen-in-New-Zealand rolls, and adapted it to what you find here.

It's not an especially difficult yeast project, as there's no kneading or punching down. But you do need to allow time, as the dough rises overnight in the fridge and again once you've shaped the individual rolls.

You'll have your little mushroom-shaped buns, and they'll be buttery with a nice, light flavor. Knock yourself out.

Butterflake Rolls
Makes 1 dozen

1 package dry yeast (1 scant tablespoon)
$^3/_4$ cup lukewarm water (100 to 105 degrees)
$^1/_4$ cup sugar
2 cups flour
1 teaspoon salt
2 eggs, beaten
$^1/_4$ cup vegetable shortening, melted
$^1/_4$ cup butter, melted

Combine yeast, water and sugar, stir; let sit 5 minutes.

Sift together flour and salt.

Beat eggs with shortening; add yeast mixture. Stir in flour mixture gradually.

Cover and refrigerate overnight or as long as a week. (Be sure your container is large enough to let dough rise to almost double.)

Next morning roll out dough to about $^3/_4$-inch thickness and brush with butter. Fold over. Roll out and fold again three times, brushing with butter each time.

Cut into 12 1$^1/_2$ inch squares. Place in muffin tins. Brush with more butter. Let rise 2 hours.

Preheat oven to 400 degrees. Bake rolls 10 minutes.

Priming the Palate 33

February 14, 2007

On Sunday we enter the Year of the Boar. Boar equals pig. Pig equals pork. Pork equals dinner. The new year, a time of fresh starts, is a fitting occasion to learn something new, perhaps to make something you've always bought readymade because you never knew any better.

Enter: char siu and chef Steve Chiang of the Golden Dragon restaurant, whose crew makes more than twenty-five pounds of this Cantonese staple every day. He's pretty much got the technique embedded in his fingertips.

Char siu is often called Chinese barbecued pork, although it isn't barbecued in the sense of being grilled over coals or wood, but rather roasted in an oven. The name means "fork roasted," for the technique of suspending the meat on prongs while cooking.

Normally, strips of pork are hung in ovens that are longer than what you've got in your kitchen. This way, fat and excess marinade drip off the meat, which glazes evenly all around.

Chiang says you can do this at home by arranging your two oven racks in the highest and lowest positions, then using hooks to hang the meat from the top rack (try S-hooks from a hardware store, or, Chiang suggests, modified metal coat hangers). Put a sheet pan on the lower rack to catch dripping fat. You'll need to cut the meat short enough to fit in the oven.

Or, use a roasting pan. Many Chinese cookbooks call instead for laying the meat on a rack over a roasting pan. This seems a more practical option, so I've modified Chiang's recipe to take this approach.

Good char siu is slightly sweet with a deep, smoky flavor and a light red glaze. It's not greasy. Bad char siu is fatty, overly sweet and sticky. Make it yourself and you can eliminate the negatives.

The key to the dish? "Patience is very important," Chiang says. Allow enough time to fully marinate the meat. Four hours is OK, but overnight is better.

And take the time to really massage the marinade into the meat, so the flavor goes deep, Chiang says. "Think about massaging your wife."

Golden Dragon Pork Char Siu

Serves 12

5 pounds pork butt, fat trimmed

» Marinade:
1 cup sugar
2$^1/_2$ tablespoons salt
1 tablespoon five-spice powder
$^1/_4$ cup ketchup
$^1/_4$ cup hoisin sauce
1 ounce (about 1 cube) wet bean curd (see note)
2 tablespoons sesame oil
2 tablespoons brandy
$^1/_4$ teaspoon red food coloring

Cut pork lengthwise into 1-inch thick slices, about 2 inches wide. Cover in water and soak 1 hour to draw out blood.

Combine marinade ingredients, breaking up bean curd and stirring until well-combined.

Drain pork well.

Cover with marinade and mix well with hands a few minutes, so meat is well-coated and to work in flavor. Cover and refrigerate 4 hours to overnight.

Preheat oven to 350 degrees.

Place pork on a rack over a roasting pan. Roast 45 minutes.

Golden Dragon char siu ingredients include brandy, seasame oil, wet bean curd, hoison sauce and ketchup.

Reduce oven heat to 300, turn meat and roast 20 minutes longer.

NOTE: Wet bean curd is made of tofu cubes preserved in wine and salt. It is common in Chinese roast duck, chicken and spare ribs. Find it sold in 16-ounce jars for about $2 in most Chinatown groceries.

Priming the Palate « 35

February 6, 2008

I believe in keeping an open mind about food. Organ meat, brains, fermented whatever—I'll try anything once. But this week's recipe at first glance was just weird.

Now, tell me if this doesn't sound a little strange: the recipe includes garlic, five-spice, candied wintermelon and (the yummiest part) red fermented bean curd. But think of it as a biscuit and not a sweet cookie. Keep an open mind.

The pastry in question is called a Little Chicken Cookie—Gai Dsai Biang, or Kai Chai Peang in Chinese.

Published recipes are very similar, and I offer an adapted version here, based on my testing. Despite the challenging nature of the ingredients, it is a pretty good, savory treat.

The ingredients can be found in Chinatown groceries. I thought maltose was going to be a deal-breaker, but I found it in little plastic tubs in several markets. I wouldn't use it again, though. It's hopelessly sticky and hard to work with. Given the small amount used, I'd just substitute brown sugar.

Little Chicken Biscuits

Makes about 2 dozen

2 cups flour
1 teaspoon baking powder
$^1/_2$ teaspoon salt
$^1/_2$ teaspoon pepper
$^1/_2$ teaspoon Chinese five-spice powder
$1^1/_2$ teaspoons minced garlic
2 pieces nam yue (red fermented bean curd)
$^1/_2$ cup vegetable oil
2 eggs, lightly beaten
2 tablespoons maltose or brown sugar
$^1/_2$ cup sesame seeds
$^3/_4$ cup minced candied wintermelon (about 12 pieces)

Preheat oven to 350 degrees. Line cookie sheets with parchment paper.

Combine flour, baking powder, salt, pepper, five-spice and garlic.

Mash bean curd and combine with oil, eggs and maltose or brown sugar. Add to dry ingredients and knead lightly. Sprinkle with sesame seeds and wintermelon; mix to incorporate evenly. Knead until mixture holds together (if it's too dry, add a little more oil).

Form dough into 1-inch balls. Place between sheets of parchment and flatten with rolling pin, or press with your palm, to $^1/_8$-inch thickness. Make them a little thicker if you want them chewier. If edges get crumbly, press them in to form a nice circle.

Place on cookie sheets and bake 15 to 20 minutes, until brown and crisp. Let cool slightly, then carefully move to wire rack to cool completely.

Priming the Palate « 37

December 20, 2006

Most things at Side Street Inn are simple, but if you've got a hankering for the restaurant's famed Garlic Edamame, you're in for a little more complicated experience.

Owner Colin Nishida explained the process: First, you make a compound butter, which means smooshing seasonings into a block of softened butter. They make the butter in huge amounts at Side Street and scoop it out as needed, so Nishida approximated the proportions in the recipe that follows.

This means you shouldn't expect your results be an exact match, but I tried it—and it is seriously good. Take some to a potluck and everyone will ask how you did it.

Variations would be easy: If you want something spicier, for example, use more hot sauce and throw in some chili flakes.

This recipe calls for 2 pounds of soy beans, but if you choose to make only 1 pound, I'd suggest you still make the full amount of compound butter. The leftover can be used to sauté vegetables, flavor grilled seafood, or make garlic bread.

Side Street Inn Garlic Edamame

2 pounds soy beans in pods
2 tablespoons olive oil
6 cloves garlic, minced
Lemon wedge

» **Compound butter:**
1 stick (1/2 cup) butter, at room temperature
1 tablespoon minced garlic
1 teaspoon minced shallots
1/4 teaspoon Worcestershire sauce
1/4 teaspoon hot pepper sauce
1 tablespoon lemon juice
Pinch parsley

Boil soy beans in well-salted water, about 10 minutes. Drain.

TO MAKE COMPOUND BUTTER: Combine all ingredients and mix well.

Melt compound butter in wok or large skillet over medium heat. Add olive oil and garlic. Sauté until garlic begins to brown. Turn off heat and add soy beans. Toss to coat. Finish with a squeeze of lemon.

February 18, 2004

Cornflakes make a quick and crunchy coating for shrimp, one that adds a natural corn flavor as well.

This version is served as part of the weekend lunch special at L'Uraku restaurant. Chef Hiroshi Fukui serves his deep-fried shrimp over a salad, then tops it all with a salsa of tomatoes, Maui onion and fresh corn kernels.

L'Uraku Crunchy Shrimp with Tomato Lomi

Oil for deep-frying
6 large shrimp, peeled, deveined and butterflied
Potato starch
1 egg white
1/2 cup crushed cornflakes

» **Tomato Lomi:**
1 small tomato, diced (use outer flesh only, discard pulp and seeds)
1/4 small Maui onion, minced
2 tablespoons fresh corn kernels, blanched
1/4 teaspoon fish sauce
1 tablespoon lemon juice
3 tablespoons olive oil
Pinch each salt and pepper

Heat oil to 350 degrees.

Dip each shrimp in potato starch, then egg white, then coat well in cornflakes. Fry 2 to 3 minutes, until golden. Don't undercook or the coating will be soggy. Shake off excess oil and drain on paper towels.

TO MAKE LOMI: Toss together tomato, onion and corn. In another bowl, whisk fish sauce, lemon juice and olive oil to make a vinaigrette. Toss vinaigrette with tomato mixture. Season with salt and pepper.

Top shrimp with a spoon of lomi. Serve over finely shredded lettuce, if desired.

October 13, 1999

Garlic is audacious, sometimes obnoxious, always in your face. If it were a child, it would be the one with the loud voice who never naps—impossible to ignore, but with an artistic streak that portends a creative future.

And when it comes to loving garlic, we in Hawai'i are at the forefront. Costco stores in Hawai'i, for example, bring in 5,000 pounds of garlic per week—a combination of fresh garlic in three-pound bags and peeled garlic in three-pound jars. The national average is half that.

We do love our cloves.

In a small space on Wai'alae Avenue called Ninniku-ya, chef Eiyuki Endo indulges a love of garlic unusual for someone from Japan. The only traditional Japanese dish that uses garlic, Endo said, is katsuo no tataki, grilled rare aku layered with sliced garlic and green onions and served with ponzu. Otherwise, garlic is too powerful a flavoring for a cuisine that values fresh, simple flavors over more robust ones.

Endo still managed to develop an attraction to garlic as a child, and this grew during a visit to Italy, where he discovered that the flavors he was enjoying so much had their roots in garlic.

His first Ninniku-ya (the name means "garlic") opened in 1983 in Tokyo, a fifteen-seat restaurant serving Chinese and Thai dishes."At that time, garlic wasn't popular in Japan," Endo said through interpreter Jan Masuda.

He learned to cook with it through the chefs he hired, chefs experienced in Chinese, Spanish and Italian cuisines. And Japanese diners responded. The restaurant was so successful it spawned Endo's three-story second restaurant and a number of unauthorized copy-cats throughout the country.

Hawai'i's Ninniku-ya opened two years ago with a menu heavy on pastas and "hot-stone" steaks—filets cooked and served on slabs of marble; lamb and 'ahi are also prepared this way. Endo also serves ice cream with a caramelized garlic clove. Every day the restaurant goes through 25 pounds of "regular American garlic."

He believes in garlic because of its ability to so thoroughly affect the taste of a dish. A little bit on a steak will change its flavor, he said. "Even in a soup broth it will just turn the taste totally."

This appetizer from Ninniku-ya is served with garlic toast. It's a blend of cheese and cream, mixed with 'ahi and blended, of course, with garlic.

Ninniku-ya 'Ahi Mascarpone
Serves 4 as an appetizer

$^1/_2$ **pound 'ahi, in $^1/_2$-inch-square pieces**
2 teaspoons olive oil
1 clove garlic, minced

» **Cheese mixture:**
  3 tablespoons mascarpone cheese
  2 tablespoons whipping cream
  1 tablespoon chopped green onion
  $^1/_2$ teaspoon wasabi paste
  1 clove garlic, minced

Combine 'ahi with olive oil and garlic. Set aside.

Combine cheese mixture ingredients; whip together. Fold in 'ahi. Serve on garlic toast.

Priming the Palate « 41

September 21, 2005

If your interest is in fusion cuisine, perhaps the most versatile tool among traditional lū'au foods is kālua pork. It's smoky and full of flavor, so use a little or a lot—either way you'll make an impression.

Kālua pork shows up frequently in Mexican-style dishes, as it seems to pair well with tortillas and the sweet-tanginess of salsa.

At Don Ho's Island Grill, the menu includes a Kālua Quesadilla. Such a snack would be easy to pull off at home with store-bought kālua. Simply fold a tortilla around some pork and cheese, and top with your favorite salsa.

The key to the Don Ho's version is the barbecue sauce, and the key to that is puréed guava. It's a creative mix of guava with garlic, ginger, cilantro and mint, plus any sweet barbecue sauce. A spoonful goes between the pork and the tortilla. If you can't get fresh guavas, try Hans Weiler Foods (847-2210) for purée by the quart.

Don Ho's Kālua Quesadilla

Serves 8

4 12-inch flour tortillas
1 cup shredded mozzarella cheese
1 cup shredded cheddar cheese
2 cups shredded prepared kālua pork
1 cup Thai sweet chili sauce (see notes)

» Guava BBQ Sauce:
$^1/_2$ cup guava purée
1 clove garlic
$^1/_2$-inch piece ginger, peeled
5 to 10 cilantro leaves
3 to 4 mint leaves
$^1/_2$ cup sweet barbecue sauce (see notes)

» Topping:
1 cup sour cream
$^1/_2$ cup milk
4 teaspoons lime juice

TO MAKE SAUCE: Place all ingredients in blender and blend on high about 30 seconds, until smooth.

Spread half of each tortilla with sauce. Top with cheeses, then kālua pork and sweet chili sauce. Fold in half, into a half-circle

Heat a dry skillet over medium heat. Fry quesadillas until crisp.

TO MAKE TOPPING: Combine ingredients. Stir vigorously until fluffy. Spoon over quesadillas.

NOTES: Thai sweet chili sauce is sold in bottles in the Asian section of most supermarkets. For the sweet barbecue sauce, use any commercial brand.

Priming the Palate « 43

August 5, 2009

I was trying to list all of the seven deadly sins and could only get as far as lust, envy, pride, gluttony and sloth. So I decided to fill in one of the remaining blanks with onion rings.

If onion rings aren't a deadly sin, they should be—beckoning with their crunchiness and sweet centers; trying to fool you into thinking they harbor nutritional qualities, since they're vegetable-oriented. You lust after them, envy others who have them. Frying them yourself makes you prideful, then gluttonous, then, after you eat them, slothlike.

But what is life without a little sin?

But before you start, a life lesson: Do you have a fire extinguisher in your kitchen? Check now, because if you don't look for it until you need it, surely it won't be there. This is experience talking.

In pursuit of this recipe, I set a small pot of oil on a gas burner out on the back porch, so as not to smell up the house. For reasons beyond my understanding of physics, chemistry or whatever governs flammability, the oil caught fire while I was getting the batter ready. We're talking flames three feet high. And of course, no fire extinguisher under the sink where I was sure I saw it last.

Operating in a low state of panic and after running through many alternatives in my mind, I decided to try smothering the flames in flour before calling 911, thinking in my confused state that explaining what happened would be embarrassing. The fire went out, but I do not recommend my approach should this happen to you. For one thing, find that fire extinguisher. For another, call 911. Sheesh, who cares if it's embarrassing?

But back to my onion rings. I tried many alternatives—soaking the onions in milk first, dusting them in flour, seasoning the batter, adding baking soda, etc.—only to settle on the simplest approach. The beer gives the batter plenty of flavor and enough bubbles to make it light.

So go ahead. But before you start, locate the fire extinguisher.

Beer-Battered Maui Onion Rings
Serves 4

2 large Maui onions
Vegetable oil, for frying

» Batter:
12 ounces dark beer
1 egg
2 teaspoons vegetable oil
1^1/$_2$ to 2 cups flour

Peel onions and slice into ^{1}/$_2$-inch rings.

Whisk together beer, egg and oil. Gradually whisk in flour to make a thick batter—but it should be smooth, not stiff.

Heat oil to 350 to 375 degrees.

Dip onion rings in batter, coating well all over. Shake off excess. Slip immediately into hot oil and deep-fry until golden. Remove with tongs or long chopsticks, tapping tongs against pot to shake excess oil from onion rings. Drain on paper towels.

Dipping sauces:

- Mince 1 anchovy fillet with 1 clove garlic and a few leaves of fresh basil. Stir into 1 cup mayonnaise and add a squeeze of lemon.

- Combine ^{1}/$_4$ cup EACH mayonnaise, sour cream and chili sauce or ketchup. If desired, add horseradish sauce and/or chili pepper flakes.

Priming the Palate   45

November 3, 1999

In the last century, this place was the Hale'iwa Hotel, a rest-and-recreation destination for refugees from Honolulu town. Then, in the mid-'40s, began the long run of the Sea View Inn, followed by the Chart House in 1990.

Today it's Haleiwa Joe's Seafood Grill (would've been Aloha Joe's but for a legal run-in with a California radio show host of the same name). It's a twenty-month-old surf 'n' turf restaurant with an incomparable view of the ocean from the point where Hale'iwa meets the sea.

Chef Mark Fitzek says the most popular entrée at Haleiwa Joe's is probably the filet mignon, but "being a seafood place, I'm most proud of the seafood dishes."

These include a crunchy appetizer of fried rock shrimp, made special by the dip. "Aioli" covers sauces made with mayonnaise; this one is flavored with prepared bloody Mary mix, horseradish and cayenne.

Popcorn Shrimp with Bloody Mary Aioli

Serves 2 to 3 as an appetizer

6 ounces rock shrimp
$^1/_2$ cup buttermilk
Vegetable oil for frying

» **Seasoned flour:**
$^1/_4$ cup flour
2 teaspoons paprika
$^1/_4$ teaspoon cayenne
$^1/_4$ teaspoon salt
$^1/_4$ teaspoon garlic powder

» **Aioli:**
$^1/_2$ cup mayonnaise
$^1/_4$ teaspoon minced garlic
1 teaspoon chopped parsley
1 teaspoon chopped roasted green bellpepper
1 teaspoon chopped sun-dried tomato
1 ounce bloody Mary mix
1 teaspoon horseradish paste
$^1/_4$ teaspoon cayenne

Marinate shrimp in buttermilk 1 hour. Combine seasoned flour ingredients. Dredge shrimp in flour. Fry about 1 minute in oil heated to 325 degrees.

TO MAKE AIOLI: Combine all ingredients. Makes about $^2/_3$ cup. Serve on the side with shrimp.

Priming the Palate « 47

December 29, 1999

Among the world's vegetables, there is one that can easily masquerade as meat. The portobello mushroom could well be a hamburger, with a juicy texture you can really bite into. Not that it tastes like a hamburger, but it seems, in certain preparations, to resemble meat more than veggie.

The portobello appetizer served at Kahala Moon by chef Kelvin Ro was one of the dishes that illustrated that point. The mushrooms were grilled, then served on toasty slices of bread and topped with garlicky sauce.

The Kahala Moon has closed, and Ro has moved on to the position of dining room instructor and manager at Kapi'olani Community College, but he dug the recipe out of his files.

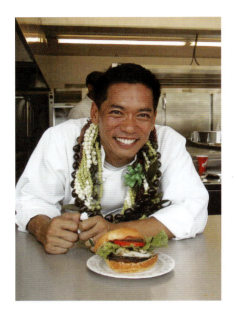

48 » Priming the Palate

Kahala Moon Fire-Roasted Portobello with Balsamic Roasted Garlic Jus

Serves 1

6 ounces chicken stock
1 tablespoon balsamic vinegar
1 tablespoon soy sauce
1 portobello mushroom
1 tablespoon olive oil
1 teaspoon roasted garlic paste (see note)
$^1/_2$ teaspoon fresh parsley, stems removed, minced
$^1/_2$ teaspoon fresh thyme, stems removed, minced
1 tablespoon butter
2 ($^1/_2$ inch) slices French bread

Prepare barbecue grill or heat oven broiler to about 400 degrees.

Combine chicken stock, balsamic vinegar and soy sauce in a saucepan. Bring to a boil, then lower heat and simmer until reduced by about one-third. Remove from heat.

Clean portobello and remove stem. Coat with olive oil. Place mushroom on grill or directly on oven rack; grill or bake until tender, about 8 to 10 minutes.

While mushroom cooks, combine the sauce reduction, roasted garlic paste and minced herbs. Bring to a simmer and stir until smooth and slightly thickened. Remove from heat, add butter and stir to incorporate.

Place bread on grill or in oven and toast until golden brown.

TO ASSEMBLE DISH: Place 1 toast slice on the other at a 90-degree angle. Slice mushroom in half and place on toast.

Bring sauce to a simmer again and stir until smooth. Pour onto the plate. Garnish with 2 roasted garlic cloves and a sprig of parsley. Serve warm.

NOTE: To prepare roasted garlic paste, remove outer skins from $^1/_2$ pound of garlic and slice bitter ends off of cloves. Place cloves in a shallow pan and cover with olive oil. Seal pan with foil and bake in 350-degree oven 20 minutes or until the garlic oil starts to sizzle. Remove from oven and cool to room temperature. Reserve 2 cloves for garnish, and strain remaining cloves to remove oil. Reserve oil for another purpose. Purée roasted garlic to form a smooth paste; if too thick, add some garlic oil. As an alternative use bottled garlic paste.

Priming the Palate   49

July 13, 2005

Quick—what does an oyster have in common with a snail?

Shells! OK, and? Basic coloring? Mushy, oozy, sliminess?

All right, so oysters and snails may never be the fairest mollusks at the ball—I read someplace that a snail is basically a head with a flattened foot. Charming. That would make an oyster a head. Period.

But there is much to love about these humble critters, especially when you throw in a whole lotta garlic and butter.

This recipe comes from the seafood buffet at Prince Court, one of several oyster dishes in the royal repertoire. It pairs oysters with escargots (snails). The escargots are sautéed in butter, garlic, lemon juice and Worcestershire sauce, then spread over the oysters.

For full restaurant effect, present the oyster shells on a bed of Hawaiian salt.

Prince Court Baked Oysters with Escargot

18 oysters
$^1/_2$ pound butter, at room temperature
$^1/_3$ cup chopped garlic
2 tablespoons lemon juice
1 tablespoon Worcestershire sauce
$^1/_2$ cup chopped parsley
Salt and white pepper, to taste
1 dozen escargot, diced
$^1/_4$ cup Hawaiian salt

Preheat oven to 350 degrees.

Shuck oysters, removing top shell. Arrange oysters in their bottom shells on a rimmed cookie sheet.

Melt butter in a saucepan; add garlic, lemon juice, Worcestershire sauce, parsley, salt and pepper. Sauté diced escargot in butter mixture. Spoon escargot and butter mixture over oysters. Bake until golden brown on top.

March 2, 2005

I always greet with trepidation requests that begin, "About thirty years ago ..." They almost always involve long-lost dishes from long-gone restaurants. Often, even the restaurant name has been lost to the past.

But there's nothing like a challenge, right? Even if the original is gone forever, sometimes a reasonable facsimile can be found.

"About thirty years ago I was able to purchase from a local Chinese restaurant a dish called Butterfly Shrimp," a reader wrote. "The shrimp was butterflied and wrapped in bacon and coated with egg and fried." She included a P.S.: "There were no snow peas with this dish."

I could see the reason for the postscript as soon as I started searching. Lots of recipes exist for Chinese butterflied shrimp and snow peas, but no bacon. In fact, the use of bacon makes this dish seem out of place as a classically Chinese dish.

The recipes I did find were on a website for Australian cooking, which could be a clue to its origin.

Butterfly Shrimp with Bacon
Serves 4

24 large shrimp
8 slices bacon, cut in thirds
$1/4$ cup vegetable oil
2 eggs, beaten

» Sauce:
3 tablespoons EACH sugar, rice vinegar and ketchup
$1/4$ teaspoon salt
$1/2$ cup water
1 teaspoon minced garlic
2 teaspoons cornstarch, dissolved in 2 tablespoons cold water

Shell and devein shrimp, leaving tails intact. Butterfly by making a slice down back, not quite all the way through. Spread halves apart and press flat. Wrap a piece of bacon around each shrimp.

Heat wok or skillet over medium heat, then add oil. Dip shrimp into beaten egg and place in wok. Fry 2 minutes, or until golden brown. Turn and fry another 2 minutes. Drain on paper towels, leaving oil in wok.

TO MAKE SAUCE: Reheat wok. Combine sugar, vinegar, ketchup, salt, water and garlic. Add to oil in wok. Bring to boil and stir in cornstarch slurry to thicken. Serve with shrimp.

Priming the Palate « 51

August 13, 2008

One of the best souvenirs of a vacation is the discovery of a new food. So it was for Glenn Takano, a recent visitor from Maryland who picked up some Tripe Poke "from a store in Wai'anae or Nānākuli somewhere."

"I am not a fan of tripe, but being an adventurous food consumer, I tasted it," Takano wrote once he got home. "Much to my surprise, it was absolutely wonderful!"

It wasn't hard to track the poke to Tamura Superette in Wai'anae, where part-owner Clifford Tamura makes a batch nearly every day for the deli. But Tamura wants to keep his recipe secret. He gave me a rough idea of the ingredients, but I'm not allowed to tell anyone else. I can safely pass on only two things:

1) He got the idea when eating a Korean tripe dish; and

2) one of the ingredients is salt.

OK, but Takano wants to make this at home, so it was on to a more effusive source: Chef Sam Choy. "That one is my favorite," Choy said when I posed the question to him. "It's very, very good. I don't know why people don't eat it more." He doesn't serve it in his restaurants, but makes it for potlucks and tailgating.

Tripe Poke doesn't fit the usual image of poke: raw seafood, usually 'ahi, mixed with soy sauce, ogo and onions. The beef tripe is cooked, which takes some long simmering, then chilled down and mixed with Korean-style flavorings.

It qualifies as poke in the loosest sense—the word is Hawaiian for slicing or cutting, and the tripe is cut into pieces, so there you go.

Choy says he uses book tripe, also called bible or leaf tripe, which cooks faster than honeycomb or blanket tripes. He says the other types have more flavor, but "you boil that forever."

Along with the tripe, you'll need Korean kochujang sauce, a chili pepper paste that includes fermented soybeans. It's sold in the Asian section of most supermarkets. Choy says for a different flavor you can substitute kim chee base, which is a mixture of chilies and garlic. Korean markets offer many types of the base. Regular supermarkets sometimes carry Park's brand, sold refrigerated near the prepared kim chee.

52   » Priming the Palate

Sam Choy's Tripe Poke
Serves 8

- 1 pound beef book tripe
- 1 cup thinly sliced green onions
- 1 cup diced onion
- 1½ tablespoons roasted sesame seeds
- 1 tablespoon sesame oil
- 1 to 2 Hawaiian chili peppers, minced
- 1½ tablespoons Korean kochujang sauce
- 1 tablespoon (or less) sugar
- 1 tablespoon soy sauce
- ½ teaspoon vinegar or lime juice

Simmer tripe in water until soft enough to pierce with your finger. Rinse in cold water. Slice and chill well, overnight if possible.

Combine with onions, sesame seeds, sesame oil and chilies.

In separate bowl, combine kochujang sauce, sugar, soy sauce and vinegar. Stir this sauce into tripe mixture.

Priming the Palate

Salads and Sides

Unless you are in the business of feeding pure carnivores–lions, for instance–your main dish will need a supporting cast. Salads and sides add color and variety to a meal, not to mention beta-carotenes, fiber and vitamin D. They make the table look pretty, too.

Now, we're not just talking rice to sop up the gravy. You know you have to do better than that. Don't make your entrée come to the party alone.

May 10, 2000

With this dish, it's all in the equipment. If you have a good quality vegetable shredder, Angelo Pietro's signature salad made from raw potatoes is a snap. Otherwise, you're going to need extremely good knife skills.

Manager Earl "Bo" Guillermo says restaurant cooks cut the potatoes by hand for the first year, but the current process is made faster and a lot more fun by an electric shredder. The machine turns out thin ribbons of potato and daikon 2 to 4 inches long, which resemble the shredded radish you'll find under your sashimi in Japanese restaurants.

To do this at home, consider buying a hand-crank shredder. Marukai has one type; Shirokiya has several selling for up to $90.

The key—beyond the shredder—is to soak the shredded potato in water to prevent browning and make it crisp. Use any dressing on the salad, but, of course, Guillermo suggests the restaurant's own line.

Angelo Pietro Raw Potato Salad
Serves 4

4 large russet potatoes
¾ pound daikon
4 large leaves iceberg lettuce, shredded
Radish and alfalfa sprouts for garnish
Angelo Pietro salad dressing (see note)

Peel potatoes and daikon, cut off ends and slice each piece lengthwise half-way through (do not split the pieces). This keeps the slices from getting too long.

Using a hand-crank or electric vegetable shredder, shred the potatoes and daikon. Place the shreds immediately into a bowl of water. Rinse until water runs clear to remove starch and prevent oxidation and browning.

Refrigerate overnight, soaked in water. If serving immediately, submerge in ice water for 5 minutes to crisp potatoes.

To serve, drain well. Place a mound of the potato-daikon mix atop a bed of lettuce. Garnish with sprouts and serve with dressing on the side.

NOTE: Angelo Pietro salad dressings in Shoyu, Ume and Sesame-Miso flavors are sold at the restaurant and most supermarkets. If desired, substitute your favorite dressing.

June 8, 2005

We have hit salad season, which means it is prime time for a main-dish mix of veggies, with added protein for bulk.

Perfect season for Niçoise, a French salad that typically involves green beans, tomatoes, black olives, anchovies, tuna and hard-boiled eggs, making it practically a one-dish meal.

Rules are made to be broken, though, and Niçoise is one of those dishes that has been adapted to many culinary styles. The venerable *Joy of Cooking* notes: "This recipe from the South of France is often carried to the point of agreeable anarchy."

The Kahala Mandarin Oriental's Plumeria Beach House offers a Niçoise that trades eggs and anchovies for slices of seared 'ahi. Now that's typical in Island versions of the dish—the real twist here is in cubes of kabocha, a small, green-skinned pumpkin easy to find in supermarkets.

Chef Milan Drager says he added the kabocha "to give Niçoise an Island touch."

Plumeria Beach House Salad Niçoise

Serves 2

$^1/_2$ cup EACH diced red bliss potatoes, diced kabocha, green beans and sliced red onions
2 tomatoes
6 ounces 'ahi
2 tablespoons olive oil
2 tablespoons blackening spice (Paul Prudhomme brand recommended)
$^1/_2$ cup kalamata olives

» Vinaigrette:
$^3/_4$ cup extra virgin olive oil
$^1/_4$ cup tablespoons balsamic vinegar
2 cloves garlic, minced
Salt and pepper, to taste

Preheat oven to 375 degrees. Roast potatoes and kabocha squash 15 minutes, or until tender.

Blanch beans and onions; cool in an ice bath. Drain.

Cut outer flesh of tomato away from seeds and pulp. Cut flesh into strips.

Heat olive oil in skillet over high heat. Coat 'ahi in blackening spice. When pan is very hot, add 'ahi and sear, 2 to 5 seconds per side. Cool and slice.

TO MAKE VINAIGRETTE: Whisk together olive oil, balsamic vinegar and garlic. Add salt and pepper.

Toss beans, potatoes, onions and squash with vinaigrette; season with salt and pepper. Top with 'ahi, olives and tomato.

Salads and Sides « 57

April 18, 2001

Chef Hector Morales at the Palm Terrace restaurant at the Turtle Bay Resort serves a simple lunch dish, Curried Chicken Salad. The salad is quickly thrown together if you have some grilled chicken on hand; Morales serves it in a papaya.

Palm Terrace Curried Chicken Salad with Papaya
Serves 4

3 chicken breasts
1/2 cup prepared mango chutney
1/2 cup diced celery
1/2 cup raisins
1/2 cup mayonnaise
3 tablespoons curry powder
Salt and pepper to taste
2 papayas, cut in half lengthwise and seeded
Cherry tomato wedges, for garnish

Grill chicken breasts until done. Set aside to cool. Dice into cubes.

In a mixing bowl, combine chicken with rest of ingredients, except papaya, and mix thoroughly. Chill in refrigerator for one hour.

Scoop chicken mixture into each papaya half. Garnish with tomatoes.

July 8, 2008

Kelaguen is a traditional side dish native to the island of Guam that can be made with raw fish (as in ceviche, the fish "cooks" in the lemon juice), raw slices of beef (same principal) or cooked crab or shrimp. The standard, though, is mannok, or chicken.

Kelaguen is a staple of the Guamanian fiesta (a party held for almost any reason). The chicken can be cooked any way—we sometimes use a rotisserie chicken from Costco—but the best kelaguen is made from chicken off the barbecue grill. The end result is like a chicken salad, but very lemony and spiced with chili peppers.

This recipe comes from Serafina Sanchez, a former caterer on Guam who now works in Honolulu for Guam Medical Referral. She'd normally start with five whole chickens and assemble the dish by taste, not measurement, so she estimated this small-quantity recipe over the phone. It squares with those you'll find in Guam cookbooks.

For best results, you'll want to use the optional grated coconut, although Sanchez says she usually doesn't. Fresh coconut spoils easily, so the dish would have to be kept chilled, she said.

And working with a whole coconut can be a lot of trouble. A good alternative, though, is frozen grated coconut from the Philippines. Look for it in Asian markets. I found a bag at Pacific Supermarket in Waipahu.

Chicken Kelaguen
Serves 8 to 10

5 pounds chicken pieces, grilled or broiled
$1/2$ medium onion, chopped
3 green onion stalks, chopped
3 small red chili peppers, crushed, or more to taste
Salt, to taste
Grated meat from $1/2$ coconut, optional
Juice from 3 to 5 lemons

Debone chicken and remove most of the skin. Cut meat into $1/2$-inch chunks. If chicken is still warm, let cool before continuing. Chicken may be prepared to this point a day ahead and refrigerated.

Combine with remaining ingredients, adding lemon juice last, to taste.

NOTE: If using coconut, keep dish cold at all times or the coconut will spoil.

August 16, 2000

Rarely do you hear someone enamored of a salad dressing, but when a request came in for the house salad dressing at Mediterraneo, the wording was unequivocal. "Everyone loved it.... It was unlike any other salad dressing I've ever tasted."

Fabrizzio Favale opened Mediterraneo seven years ago, following partnerships with Sergio Mitrotti at Cafe Cambio and Cafe Sistina. His restaurant, between Pi'ikoi and Ke'eaumoku, is just down King Street from Cafe Sistina.

Cooking runs in the family, beginning with Favale's mother, who started him on this path. "My mom is unbelievable, a classic Italian lady. Everything she touch, come good." His two sisters run a restaurant in Rome.

True Italian food showcases quality ingredients, without fanciness or pretense, Favale says. "In Rome we eat very simple things, but the quality got to be good. The restaurant got to be simple."

His dressing recipe is indeed simple. Simple enough that he dictated it as he cooked, rather than write it down. Watch him in the kitchen and he's not measuring anything, anyway. Taste as you go, he says.

As for technique, well, with the salad the key is being hands-on. He has his cooks toss the greens with their hands, and taste every portion after salting to be sure the mix is right.

The greens are flavored first with olive oil, red wine vinegar and salt, then topped with a dressing of chopped tomatoes marinated in garlic, olive oil and basil. No balsamic vinegar, which makes him throw up his hands and roll his eyes. At Mediterraneo, balsamic is deemed worthy only as a dip for bread.

Mediterraneo Salad
Serves 4

1 lettuce heart
4 cups mixed greens
4 tablespoons extra virgin olive oil
1 tablespoon red wine vinegar
Salt to taste

» **Dressing:**
2 tablespoons olive oil
1 clove garlic, chopped
10 basil leaves, chopped fine
$1/2$ teaspoon salt
Pinch black pepper
2 tomatoes, chopped fine

Process all dressing ingredients, except tomatoes, in a food processor or blender. Pour over tomatoes, cover and refrigerate overnight.

Break up lettuce heart and toss with greens. Just before serving, toss with oil, vinegar and salt. Use your hands and taste, adjusting seasoning. Divide among 4 plates. Top each with dressing.

Salads and Sides 61

December 20, 2000

One of the most practical pieces of advice I ever received was from a reporter who told me that conducting an interview over lunch is much easier if you order a salad—because you can eat it with your left hand and still take notes.

Makes sense, unless you happen to get one of those salads where the tomato slices are too big to fit in your mouth, or the lettuce is torn into pieces only roughly approximating "bite-sized."

A safe haven, whether you must take notes or just have knife-avoidance, is a chopped salad. Everything in this dish is smaller-than-bite-sized and coated in dressing. Nothing is left for you to do but lift the fork and chew, with no worries about a stray strip of vegetation hanging from the corner of your mouth.

A particularly popular chopped salad is served at Palomino Euro Bistro in Harbor Court.

Chef Fred DeAngelo says the salad is a favorite at the restaurant. "It's not only good as a starter; a lot of people have the entrée-size for lunch."

DeAngelo says you can give the salad variety by "adding different proteins," say, roasted or grilled chicken or even sliced duck breast. The heart of the salad is a balsamic vinaigrette made creamy by an egg yolk.

Palomino Chop Chop Salad
Serves 2

6 ounces (about 3 cups) romaine hearts, julienned
4 leaves fresh basil, julienned
2 ounces (about $1/3$ cup) provolone cheese, cubed
1 ounce (about 3 tablespoons) whole garbanzo beans
1 ounce salami, julienned
2 ounces smoked turkey breast, in $1/2$-inch pieces
2 ounces (about $1/3$ cup) diced tomato

» **Garnish:**
Pinch grated Parmesan cheese
Pepper to taste
2 basil sprigs

» **Dressing (Makes $1/2$ cup):**
1 egg yolk (pasteurized if worried about raw egg)
3 ounces (6 tablespoons) balsamic vinegar
1 roasted garlic clove, minced
Salt and pepper to taste
1 ounce (2 tablespoons) olive oil

TO MAKE DRESSING: Whip yolk to a froth. Add vinegar, garlic, salt and pepper. Continue to whip until mixture is "tight," or very well-combined. (Or, place yolk in blender and blend for 2 to 3 minutes. Add other ingredients and blend 2 to 3 minutes longer.) Drizzle in oil and continue to whip or blend until emulsified.

TO ASSEMBLE SALAD: Combine salad ingredients, reserving half the tomatoes for garnish. Toss with dressing. Garnish with remaining tomatoes, Parmesan, pepper and basil sprig.

Salads and Sides   63

June 17, 2009

The scalloped potato dish served on the brunch menu at Orchids at the Halekulani is really a masterpiece of simplicity: just five ingredients—and two of them are salt and pepper. There's no thickener (such as the flour found in most scalloped potato recipes), so there's not even any stirring involved.

Once you slice the potatoes, little effort is required; your oven will do all the work. Although the recipe calls for it, I didn't even peel the potatoes when I tested the dish—Yukon Golds have a smooth, soft skin that melts into the dish.

Why is it special? All the cheese that goes over the top has a lot to do with it. Plus the dish is chilled overnight, which allows everything to set up nicely before you slice it, reheat and serve.

My test version came out of the fridge firm and as easy to slice as a cake. Once reheated, the cream and cheese softened just a bit, into a puddle of yum.

That said, this dish is an extravagance, in calories and cost. One serving has 580 calories and 40 grams of fat. The quart of cream and real Parmesan cheese will set you back around $15 (if you're tempted to use the imitation Parmesan in the green can, remember that this is a Halekulani recipe; aim higher). The potatoes, at least, are a bargain: I got a 3-pound bag on sale for $3.50.

Well, you only live once. Eat small portions.

Orchids Scalloped Potato Gratin
Serves 10

8 Yukon Gold potatoes (about 3 pounds), peeled and thinly sliced
Salt and white pepper, to taste
1 quart (4 cups) heavy cream
2 cups grated Parmesan cheese

Preheat oven to 375 degrees.

Layer potatoes in baking pan, sprinkling with salt and pepper between layers. Pour cream over the top, making sure all the potatoes are covered. Cover pan with foil and bake 45 minutes.

Remove foil and bake another 10 minutes, until top is golden brown.

Top with cheese and return to oven until cheese browns.

Chill overnight. Cut in square portions and reheat.

September 28, 2005

Strawberries are still easy to find. Here's a way to use them in a salad combined with spinach.

The salad is served at Kona Brewing Co. restaurants in Kona and Hawai'i Kai, where it offers a touch of femininity in the masculine brewery environment.

The salad is a take on a spinach salad with walnuts—but with pungent gorgonzola cheese crumbles and macadamia nuts standing in for the walnuts. Slices of strawberry provide a sweet bit of contrast.

The vinaigrette is made with 2 cups of strawberries, blended up with the oil and vinegar.

Kona Brewing Co. Strawberry Spinach Salad
Serves 6

16 ounces washed, fresh spinach leaves
Half a small Maui onion, sliced
²/₃ cup crumbled gorgonzola cheese
¹/₃ cup diced roasted macadamia nuts
10 to 12 sliced strawberries

» Strawberry Vinaigrette (Makes 1 quart):
2 cups strawberries
¹/₂ cup white wine vinegar
¹/₄ cup sugar
2 cups olive or canola oil
2 tablespoons black sesame seeds

TO MAKE VINAIGRETTE: Blend strawberries, vinegar and sugar. When mixture is smooth, slowly add oil, continuing to blend until mixture is well-incorporated. Stir in sesame seeds.

Mound spinach in medium-sized salad bowl, top with Maui onions. Sprinkle evenly with cheese and nuts. Place strawberries over top. Drizzle with vinaigrette.

Salads and Sides « 65

December 10, 2008

If I'd known it was going to be this easy, I would've made friends with this food named Su a long time ago.

Su—that's my nickname for sunomono, Japanese-style vegetable dishes in a vinegary dressing (su). Kind of like a salad, but generally served condiment-style, the way kim chee is presented in a Korean meal. Namasu (made with cucumber) is probably the most familiar, although sunomono can be made with anything from lettuce to lotus root.

Sunomono is related to tsukemono, a general name for pickles—vegetables preserved in brine. Most common of the tsukemonos is probably takuwan (made with daikon, that elongated Asian radish). My friend Su is generally described as a simpler dish with a dressing mixed generously with raw or cooked veggies.

So in reality I have two new friends, Su and Tsu.

Getting back to my point about this being easy: dressings are usually just three to four ingredients—vinegar and sugar, with the added boost of salt, soy sauce, mirin (sweet Japanese wine) or sake. Heat it in the microwave, stir to dissolve the sugar, and it's done. To think I used to buy this stuff.

These recipes owe their origins to Rachel Laudan, author of *The Food of Paradise*; Muriel Miura, author of *Japanese Cooking Hawai'i Style*; and the ladies of Honpa Hongwanji Hawai'i Betsuin, authors of the Favorite Island Cookery series.

Takuwan
Makes about 1 quart

> **1 cup sugar**
> **³/₄ cup water**
> **3 tablespoons salt**
> **¹/₄ cup rice vinegar**
> **1 pound daikon, peeled and cut in fingertip-size pieces**
> **Chopped red chili pepper, optional**
> **Yellow food coloring, optional**

Heat sugar, water, salt and vinegar; stir to dissolve sugar. Cool.

Place daikon in glass jar. Add cooled solution, chili pepper and food coloring, if using. Solution probably won't cover all the daikon, but the daikon will release liquid and in a few hours will be submerged. Refrigerate 2 days before eating.

Pickled Radish
Makes about 1 pint

    1 bunch radish (about 2 cups trimmed and quartered)
    2 teaspoons salt
    Red food coloring, optional

» **Sweet Vinegar Sauce:**
    1/3 cup rice vinegar
    1/4 cup sake
    1/3 cup sugar
    1 teaspoons salt

Sprinkle radish with salt; let stand 30 minutes to extract liquid from radish.

Combine sauce ingredients and heat to dissolve sugar and salt. Cool.

Drain radish, rinse and squeeze out liquid, using cheesecloth if necessary. Add to sauce with a few drops food coloring, if using. Let stand 1 hour.

Hasu Sanbaizuke

    1/4 cup vinegar
    1/4 cup soy sauce
    1/2 cup sugar
    1 pound lotus root, peeled and thinly sliced
    1/8 cup sliced ginger

Heat vinegar, soy sauce and sugar and simmer 5 minutes.

Add lotus root slices, turn to coat and simmer five more minutes, turning occasionally. Work in 2 batches if necessary. Liquid will reduce.

Place in glass jar with ginger and refrigerate, mixing occasionally to keep pieces coated. May be eaten immediately, or will keep several days.

Salads and Sides

April 5, 2006

A couple of months ago, I received a request for a low-carb, low-sugar version of cone sushi, with some other substance standing in for the rice—something that could be prepared for a friend with diabetes.

It was an interesting query, and Melanie Okazaki came through with suggestions based on her own experiments on stuffed aburage.

Now, stuffed aburage and cone sushi are different animals, although related in that the wrappers are both soy bean-based.

Aburage is a puffy, fried cube that needs to be boiled. It can be cut up and eaten as is, or slit and stuffed, one common filling being ground pork.

The inarizushi (cone sushi) wrapper is a thin rectangle or triangle that comes ready to use in packets or cans. All you have to do is squeeze out the liquid it's packed in.

This recipe adapts one of Okazaki's recipes into a cone sushi-like creation. Our nutritionist, Joannie Dobbs, says she'd actually add some carbs in the form of a cup of brown rice for added texture, and it would still be suited to a diabetic diet.

It would make a good picnic or potluck food: easy to eat and good warm, at room temperature, or even cold.

Inari Tuna-Tofu

16 inarizushi (cone sushi) wrappers

» **Filling:**
   1 20-ounce block firm tofu
   1 6-ounce can tuna, well drained
   ¼ cup minced green onion
   3 dried shiitake mushrooms, soaked, drained and minced
   4 dried shrimp, soaked, drained and minced
   1 egg
   Salt and pepper, to taste
   1 cup brown rice, optional

TO MAKE FILLING: Remove water from tofu by wringing in cheesecloth. Place in a mixing bowl and add remaining ingredients; mix well. Divide into 16 patties that will fit in sushi wrapper. (If using rice you will get more than 16.)

Spray a skillet with cooking oil spray and sauté over medium heat until each side is brown. Cool slightly.

Squeeze sushi wrappers to remove all liquid. Place a patty inside each one.

Dips 'n' Dressings

Seriously, you can make salad dressing. A little fat, a little acid, a little bit of seasoning, and you've got a custom dressing for fresh vegetables, grilled meats, whatever's on the table tonight.

A surprising number of "By Request" inquiries are for dressings, dips and sauces–things we might treat as afterthoughts. But really, they should be given way more consideration. When you make a salad, after all, Mother Nature does the work; you simply slice and toss. Your true contribution is a dressing that gives it zest.

The same could be said for the sauce on a burger–remember the yellow sauce at Andy's Drive-Inn?

Often the finishing touch is the one that lingers.

September 9, 2005

It's only a burger. A pre-made, pre-packed, pre-frozen patty on a very ordinary bun. Yet these burgers are the subject of genuine devotion, to the point that people buy them by the dozens and freeze them for later microwaving.

But it ain't the beef, people, it's the sauces.

The tangy, chunky red and yellow sauces that coat the tops and bottoms of burgers at Byron's Drive-In migrated across the island from the old Andy's Drive-In in Kailua, where they were something of a legend. "I remember when we closed, we sold gallons at Andy's," recalls Marian Wong, wife of the late restaurateur extraordinaire, Andy Wong.

Those sauces are the objects of much desire among readers of this column, who've long been after the formulas. They've also been after the recipes for clam chowder from Chowder House, braised oxtails from Byron's, peppered 'ahi from Orson's, the macaroni salad from Andy's....

All these restaurants were opened by Andy and Marian Wong over a fifty-year span that began with Andy's in 1957.

Not to get your hopes up: I have none of those recipes. Many have sought them, Marian says, but none shall receive. "The things that we make money on—cannot give the recipes."

I do have, however, very respectable facsimiles of the sauce recipes.

Reader John Stewart grew up in Kailua with a fondness for Andy's hamburgers. "Long ago I tried to analyze how the sauces were made and have been using my versions for years."

Marian Wong took a look at Stewart's formula and pronounced it "close," but that's all the hinting she'll do.

The recipes that follow are adaptations of Stewart's recipes, after side-by-side tasting with the sauces now served at Byron's. They are quite close.

Yellow Sauce
Makes about ¾ cup

½ small onion
5 tablespoons mayonnaise
1 tablespoon mustard
¼ teaspoon minced garlic (see note)

Grate enough onion to make 1 teaspoon. Chop enough of the rest to make 3 tablespoons (about ⅛-inch pieces, but they can be uneven in size).

Combine mayonnaise, mustard, garlic and onions, including juice from grated onion. Chill well.

NOTE: It's best to use prepared, minced garlic—the type that comes in a jar or squeeze tube. The milder flavor and smooth consistency merge better in the sauce.

Red Sauce

½ cup ketchup
¼ cup sweet pickle relish

Combine ingredients. Chill well.

Marian Wong holds a photo of her late husband, Andy, while showing off some of the plate-lunch specialities from Byron's Drive-In. Marian and Andy opened a number of restaurants, beginning with Andy's Drive-In in Kailua.

September 4, 2002

For people with food allergies, eating out is an adventure that doesn't always end well.

It's not that restaurants aren't sympathetic. Most chefs are quite willing to accommodate the needs of those allergic to nuts, dairy or wheat products—or all of those things. But mistakes can happen when a chef doesn't realize that soy sauce contains wheat, or that a trace amount of butter or nuts in a pan can trigger trouble.

And then there's the meal itself: broiled fish or chicken and steamed vegetables are the norm. A restaurant meal is just not the gourmet delight that it is for others at the table.

But Aaron's Atop the Ala Moana offers a vinaigrette with capers that's safe for most sensitive people—even though it was created for general use, not to accommodate food allergies.

George Gomes, executive chef for the Tri-Star Restaurant Group that owns Aaron's, says the dressing is used in various ways within the chain and works well as a dressing for grilled chicken or fish. At Sarento's Top of the "I" it's served with an artichoke and tomato salad; at Nick's Fishmarket Maui with the Maui Wowie Salad.

"People love that dressing; they use it on different things. It's very versatile."

Aaron's Caper Vinaigrette
Makes about 4 cups

1 roasted red bell pepper, skinned, seeded and chopped (see note)
2 tablespoons capers
$1/2$ teaspoon chopped garlic
1 tablespoon chopped fresh oregano
1 tablespoon chopped fresh parsley
Whites from 2 hard-boiled eggs
$1^1/_2$ cups red wine vinegar
$1^1/_2$ cups extra virgin olive oil
Salt and pepper to taste

Combine all ingredients except oil, salt and pepper. Add oil gradually while whisking lightly to emulsify. Adjust taste with salt and pepper.

NOTE: To roast bell pepper, place whole pepper on a grill or under a broiler, turning until all the skin is charred. Place in paper bag until cool enough to handle. Remove skin under running water, then discard seeds and stem. Commercially prepared roasted bell peppers are also available in jars in most supermarkets.

November 18, 2009

If you've never made your own cranberry sauce, enlightenment awaits. Do-it-yourself cranberry sauce is probably the single easiest item you could add to your Thanksgiving repertoire. It will be nothing like that tube-shaped gelatinous thing that plops out of a can. Yours will have taste, texture and tartness—perfect for dressing up the turkey and fixings next week.

Why try? Let us count the reasons:

- It's simple. Place one bag of cranberries in a pot with water and sugar (the proportions are given on the bag). Simmer until the berries pop. Pau.

- It can be done ahead. Refrigerate the sauce till turkey day. In the meantime you can serve spoonfuls along with anything you're eating, from roast meats to curries to plain toast.

- You don't even need a stove. Toss the ingredients in a slow cooker and let it go for a couple of hours while you go about the many tasks that this time of year can bring.

- You can make it your own. For one thing, you can control the amount of sugar. Beyond that, fancy it up with spices (cinnamon or ginger are naturals), additional fruits (orange is traditional) or pour in wine or apple cider.

This version of Thanksgiving's traditional sauce comes from the Halekulani. It's made extra-yummy with an apple, orange and pear.

Halekulani Cranberry Sauce

1 cup water
1 cup sugar
1 12-ounce package fresh cranberries
1 orange, peeled and puréed
1 apple, peeled, cored and diced
1 pear, peeled, cored and diced
$^1/_2$ teaspoon salt
1 teaspoon cinnamon
$^1/_2$ teaspoon nutmeg

In a medium saucepan, bring water to boil. Add sugar and stir to dissolve.

Reduce heat to simmer; stir in remaining ingredients. Cover and simmer 30 minutes, stirring occasionally, until cranberries burst. Cool to room temperature.

Dips 'n' Dressings « 73

July 6, 2005

Anchovies used to be high on my hate list, but now that I am older and wiser, I am enamored of them. One of my favorite meals—do not be alarmed—is anchovies and poi. So when a reader asked for a recipe for an anchovy vinaigrette, I was willing to dig in for some trial and error.

Anchovies are the basis of two classic dressings, Caesar and Green Goddess. Vinaigrettes are less common, but I did find a few recipes and started whisking.

The common ingredients were oil, vinegar, mustard powder and lemon juice, plus anchovies in greater or lesser quantities. Basic Caesars are similar, although the classics also have a raw egg and lots of garlic. The version below makes about enough for a dinner's worth of salad for a family of four.

The basic formula is easily modified to add your favorite fresh herbs, a splash of wine—or maybe some poi.

Anchovy Salad Dressing
Makes ¹/₂ cup

3 anchovy fillets, minced
1 teaspoon anchovy oil
¹/₄ cup olive oil
2 tablespoons red wine vinegar
1 tablespoon lemon juice
1 clove garlic, minced
1 tablespoon minced onion
¹/₂ teaspoon dry mustard
¹/₄ teaspoon pepper
1 teaspoon sugar

Whisk ingredients together until oil is emulsified. Or place in covered jar and shake.

74   » Dips 'n' Dressings

November 16, 2005

In a theatrical context, the Green Goddess is the spiritual crutch of the Rajah of Rukh. In a cooking context, the Green Goddess is mayonnaise, anchovies and tarragon, and especially good on seafood.

Culinary references agree on the dressing's source: the Palace Hotel in San Francisco in the 1920s. A famed British stage star, George Arliss, was staying at the Palace while performing in the city in a play called *The Green Goddess*.

Arliss played the rajah of a potentate near India, into which crashed a small plane bearing three British citizens. They survived, but the rajah refused to help them, believing that the Green Goddess had sent them to atone for certain injustices perpetrated by England against him.

"Asia has a long score against you swaggering lords," is one of his lines.

Anyway, the hotel dedicated a dressing to Arliss and the play (a nice entrée might have been more of a tribute, but perhaps the idea of a green spiritual being turned thoughts to salad).

The classic dressing is an easy mix of mayonnaise, anchovies and vinegar, with the green coming from the herbs tarragon, parsley and chives. It actually turns out white with flecks of green, although some commercial preparations use food coloring to make it worthy of the name. Variations on the basic formula add sour cream, lemon juice or garlic.

The dressing became the signature of the Palace Hotel, where it was often served with seafood. It can be used as a dip as well, and makes a good base for coleslaw.

Green Goddess Dressing
Makes a little more than 1 cup

1 tablespoon minced green onion or chives
1 tablespoon minced parsley
$1/4$ to $1/2$ teaspoon dried tarragon, crushed, or 1 teaspoon fresh, minced
4 anchovy fillets
2 tablespoons oil from anchovies
1 cup mayonnaise
1 tablespoon white wine or tarragon vinegar
1 tablespoon lemon juice

Combine green onion, parsley, tarragon and anchovies on a cutting board and mince anchovies into the herbs, forming a paste. Or crush ingredients together with a mortar and pestle.

Combine remaining ingredients, then add anchovy mixture and mix.

Dips 'n' Dressings

January 16, 2008

Hari Kojima has been long gone from local television, but memories of his *Let's Go Fishing* and *Hari's Kitchen* shows from the 1980s and '90s remain strong.

Kojima left KHON and both his shows in 1998 and now works for the seafood wholesaler Fresh Island Fish. He's said he prefers to leave television to the new generation.

His *Hari's Kitchen* heritage is a collection of recipes that are easy crowd-pleasers, such as this crab dip, from a cookbook that Kojima wrote with Muriel Miura in 1994, *Cooking with Hari & Muriel*. The slim paperback, self-published and long out of print, opens with Kojima's familiar, "Hi gang!"

His dip is easy to assemble, using the creamy trio of cream cheese, mayonnaise and cream of mushroom soup. A bit of unflavored gelatin is added and it goes into a mold (a small Jell-O mold or mini bundt pan would produce a decorative end-product, although you could also just pack it into a bowl).

Let it set in the refrigerator, then unmold, surround it with crackers, and make it the centerpiece of a finger-food table. It makes enough for a party.

To simplify, leave out the gelatin and simply place the dip in a bowl.

One tip: The most time-consuming part is grating a cup of celery. If you've never done this before (I hadn't), the advantage is that it gets rid of all the strings. The disadvantage is that celery is so watery and porous that the stalks sort of collapse against the grater and you've got to watch out for your knuckles. Lots of water comes out, so be sure to squeeze it dry before adding it to the crab mixture.

Also, obviously you get the best results with the best quality crabmeat. You'll find a big price difference between the usual canned stuff and premium chunky grades. The cheap stuff does produce a good dip, but if you want a hefty crab flavor to stand up to all that cream-cheesiness, you'll have to put up the bucks.

Hari Kojima's King Crab Dip

- 8 ounces cream cheese
- 1 14.5-ounce can cream of mushroom soup
- 1 cup mayonnaise
- 1 8-ounce can crabmeat, drained well
- 1 cup grated celery, with excess water squeezed out
- 7 stalks green onion, minced
- Salt and pepper, to taste
- 1 package unflavored gelatin
- 2 tablespoons warm water

Melt cream cheese in sauce pan over low heat. Add soup and mayonnaise and stir until smooth. Remove from heat. (Or combine all 3 in large bowl and microwave 1 to 2 minutes.)

Stir in crab, celery, green onion, salt and pepper.

Dissolve gelatin in water and stir into crab mixture. Place in greased mold. Chill overnight.

Unmold onto platter and serve with crackers.

October 15, 2003

A good dressing is the difference between a "blah" bowl of greens and a salad that's worth writing home about.

These two come from Kaka'ako Kitchen. One is a creamy bleu cheese dressing, the other a vinaigrette.

Marsha Cades, chef at Kaka'ako Kitchen, provided both recipes. She said the Balsamic Vinaigrette is an especially great dressing that also makes a good marinade.

Both recipes were for large quantities and have been reduced here, although the bleu cheese dressing still makes 4 cups. Save it for when you need to impress a salad-eating crowd.

Kaka'ako Kitchen Basil-Bleu Cheese Dressing

Makes about 4 cups

1/4 cup chopped basil
1 clove garlic
1/2 cup vinegar
2 1/2 teaspoons Dijon mustard
6 tablespoons honey
Juice of 1/2 lemon
1/4 cup mayonnaise
3/4 cup crumbled bleu cheese
1 1/2 cups vegetable oil
Salt and pepper, to taste

Combine basil, garlic and vinegar; set aside for 10 minutes to allow the acid in the vinegar to bring out the flavors in the herbs. Place all ingredients except oil in a blender and blend until well-combined. Slowly add oil and blend until mixture is creamy. Season to taste with salt and pepper.

Kaka'ako Kitchen Balsamic Vinaigrette

Makes about 2 cups

1/2 cup balsamic vinegar
1/4 cup chopped basil
1 1/2 teaspoons minced garlic
1 teaspoon pepper
1 1/2 cups olive oil

Combine all ingredients except oil in a bowl and whisk. Slowly add oil and whisk to emulsify.

March 19, 2003

Sometimes the crucial element in a dish is not the central ingredient, but an embellishment. A tangy sauce or a crispy garnish can be the detail that demands attention.

Such is the case with the Duck Napoleons served by the Renaissance Ilikai Hotel during a recent Brunch on the Beach in Waikīkī. The dish consisted of shredded cooked duck, diced tomatoes and baby greens topped with a vinaigrette flavored with hoisin sauce. At home you could assemble a reasonable facsimile: a simple salad topped with duck and the vinaigrette. Top with crunchy won ton chips to seal the effect.

This would also make a nice change-of-pace dipping sauce for the next time you roast duck.

Ilikai Hoisin Vinaigrette
Makes about 3 cups

3^1/$_2$ tablespoons sake
1^1/$_2$ tablespoons minced fermented black beans
2^1/$_2$ tablespoons vegetable oil
2 scant tablespoons EACH minced garlic, minced ginger and finely sliced green onion
1^3/$_4$ cups hoisin sauce
1^1/$_2$ tablespoons plum sauce
^{1}/$_2$ cup orange juice, with pulp
1^3/$_4$ cups rice vinegar

Combine sake and black beans; let stand 10 minutes.

Heat oil in a heavy pan over low heat. Add garlic, ginger and green onion. Stir until softened, about 10 minutes. Remove from heat. Add remaining ingredients and stir to blend.

Dips 'n' Dressings   79

March 10, 1999

Many people—many, many, many people, actually—consider the mango chutney sold at the Punahou Carnival to be the best chutney on the planet. This chutney has so many fans that it usually sells out in a few hours, or at the latest by the end of the first day.

It is a wonderfully chunky chutney, tart with a spicy bite that comes from just a few small red peppers.

Bonnie Judd, director of communications at Punahou, provided this recipe, plus these facts and figures about the famous Punahou chutney:

The recipe falls within the purview of the Jams and Jellies Booth and has changed over the years with the availability of mangoes and the imagination of the booth chairpersons. This year's committee made six thousand jars of chutney, as well as jars of mango sauce; liliko'i and guava butter; and jellies of red pepper, green pepper, jaboticaba, Surinam cherry, guava and liliko'i.

Punahou seeks donations of mangoes through the summer, when the chutney is cooked and canned. If you are loaded with mangoes, the school will send volunteers to help you pick them.

If you have no mango source, or if this recipe just looks like too much trouble for you, the carnival is held on the first Friday and Saturday in February.

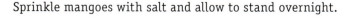

Punahou Mango Chutney
Makes 15 pints

- 10 pounds mangoes (green or half-ripe), peeled, sliced and cut in chunks
- 3/4 cups salt
- 5 pounds sugar
- 6 or 7 cups cider vinegar, depending on acidity of mangoes
- 1 1/2 pounds almonds, blanched and cut in thin strips
- 1 pound finely sliced candied lemon peel
- 1 pound finely sliced candied orange peel
- 2 large onions, chopped fine
- 2 pounds seedless raisins
- 1 pound finely sliced candied citron
- 2/3 cup green ginger, cooked and chopped fine
- 1 cup finely chopped preserved ginger
- 2 cloves garlic, chopped fine
- 8 small Hawaiian chilis, with seeds removed, chopped fine

Sprinkle mangoes with salt and allow to stand overnight.

Boil the sugar and vinegar 5 minutes, add to the drained mango, cook until tender. Add the other ingredients and cook slowly to desired consistency, 30 minutes to an hour. Pour into hot, sterilized jars and seal immediately.

July 14, 2004

Oka is a fish dish that approximates poke—or perhaps ceviche, but, in a way, neither.

It is a Samoan dish of raw fish and coconut milk, subject to interpretation by family tradition, the individual cook's style, and the ingredients on hand. Kind of like poke. The only essential is the coconut milk. Even the fish is sometimes substituted with other seafood.

An Internet search for oka will yield dozens of hits, but they all seem to lead back to one recipe. A version of it follows. Chopped raw mussels are suggested as a substitute for the fish.

In 1999, Iva Kinimaka of Iva's Komplete Katering made his version of oka on the KHON-TV cooking show *Hawai'i's Kitchen*. He included chopped fresh tomatoes and lemon juice, which could easily be mixed into this recipe if you enjoy those flavors.

Oka, by the way, is also the name of a soft, creamy cheese made in Canada. But I would not suggest that as an addition to this dish.

Oka with Crabmeat

3 pounds fresh 'ahi or snapper, skin and bones removed, chopped
2 cups unsweetened coconut milk
1 cup water
1 cup chopped onions
1 cup crabmeat
1 cup chopped cucumbers
Salt and pepper, to taste

Combine all ingredients in a large bowl. Refrigerate 30 minutes to an hour before eating.

July 30, 2008

The papaya, mellow in color and comforting to hold in the palm of the hand, is also very good for you. High in vitamin C, folate, potassium and lots of other happy nutrients and antioxidants, it would definitely fall on the plus side of almost any diet.

While it's perfectly good enough to simply cut your papaya in half, scoop out the seeds, then dig in with a spoon, it's nice to find another way to capitalize on its nutritional bounty.

At Mariposa at Neiman Marcus a Papaya-Champagne Vinaigrette is drizzled over an Applewood Salmon Salad that includes greens, Maui onion and goat cheese.

It's a very easy dressing to make: a relatively short list of ingredients is simply puréed smooth in a blender. Results will vary some, though, depending on the type of papaya and sparkling wine that you use.

Mariposa mixes up 5 gallons at a time, so for consistency's sake a prepared papaya purée is used—Perfect Purée, which I haven't found sold retail locally. It is available at $22.50 for 30 ounces by mail at *www.perfectpuree.com*, but really, with fresh papaya so easy to find, why would you bother?

The recipe that follows has been cut down 20 times from the original, but my trial batch using fresh papaya was a good match to one from Mariposa. The dressing is a beautiful golden color with a tart, fruity taste. Your best bet is to make the dressing according to the proportions listed here, then taste and make adjustments—probably in the vinegar and sugar.

Bonus result: You get to drink the rest of the champagne.

Mariposa Papaya-Champagne Vinaigrette
Makes about 4 cups

2¼ cups papaya purée (see note)
5 tablespoons sparkling wine
¾ cup olive oil
2½ tablespoons extra virgin olive oil
¾ cup rice wine vinegar
2½ teaspoons minced shallots
2 tablespoons sugar
Pinch thyme

Put all ingredients in blender and purée until smooth. Taste and add more vinegar or sugar if needed. Dressing should be tart.

NOTE: To make purée from fresh papaya, peel fruit and remove seeds; place chunks of fruit in blender. Purée until smooth.

March 19, 2003

Canning and caring are sure signs of spring among the ladies of the Honpa Hongwanji Hawai'i Betsuin. They've been at work for weeks, cooking down kumquats, jaboticaba and guavas-cultivated, donated- or scrounged-into preserves, jams and jellies.

In this quiet but consistent manner, the ladies have contributed in major ways not just to the social calendar of the temple, but also to its financial health. It's a function common to the women's arm of Hawaii's Hongwanji temples.

"They have been a real financial mainstay of the temple," says Mary Tanouye, temple president. "I think this is true across the state. They keep the temples going."

Not long ago, the women were able to donate $20,000 toward installing an elevator at the temple, and Tanouye says they have another $20,000 certificate of deposit about to mature.

Among the leading accomplishments of these women was the publication in 1973 of the first edition of *Favorite Island Cookery*, a collection of local-style recipes that was rare for its time. Five more volumes followed, and over the years the cookbooks have raised thousands of dollars. This cash and the sales from the annual bazaars went into safe, slow-growing CDs that upon maturity would yield a cash bonus for the temple.

This recipe from the ladies of the Betsuin is for kumquat preserves, to be sold at the bazaar. It's from cookbook number three.

Whole Kumquat Preserves

4 cups kumquats
4 tablespoons baking soda
4 thin slices lemon, optional
1 teaspoon grated ginger
3 cups water
3 cups sugar
1 cup light corn syrup

Wash kumquats and sprinkle with baking soda. Cover with water and let stand 10 minutes. Drain and wash twice. Place kumquats in pot; cover with water. Cook $1/2$ hour or until tender. Drain.

Cook lemon and ginger in a small amount of water until tender. Drain.

Combine water, sugar and corn syrup and boil 5 minutes. Add kumquats, lemon and ginger. Simmer 35 to 40 minutes or until glossy and transparent. Place in sterilized bottles and seal.

June 4, 2008

Tarragon is the herb of spring, many experienced cooks say, the way basil is for summer and rosemary is for fall.

Of those three, though, tarragon is the least familiar, and not as likely to be in the spice cabinet or growing in the garden.

So, a quick lesson:

The McCormick Spice Co.'s *EnSpicelopedia* says tarragon comes from an herb called *Artemisia dracunculus*. The English name of tarragon comes from the French word estragon, "little dragon," possibly because it was believed to cure bites of poisonous reptiles, or because it had serpent-like roots.

The herb's flavor is usually compared to licorice—or anise, in culinary parlance. It has a deep, earthy scent and flavor, and it is very strong, so very little is needed to make a point.

Tarragon pairs well with salmon, chicken, potatoes and many vegetables—especially spring favorites artichokes and asparagus. It's frequently used to flavor vinegars and in salad dressings. Green Goddess is perhaps the most familiar tarragon-based dressing. Other classic uses include Béarnaise sauce, Dijon mustard, and the "fines herbes" used in French cooking.

This simple tarragon dressing comes from Halekulani's House Without a Key, where it is served at brunch. It's a light vinaigrette that incorporates tarragon-flavored vinegar, mustard and mayonnaise.

House Without a Key Tarragon Vinaigrette
Makes about 4 cups

$^1/_2$ **cup tarragon vinegar**
6 tablespoons Dijon mustard
2 cloves garlic, chopped
6 tablespoons mayonnaise
1 tablespoon parsley, chopped
1 tablespoon fresh tarragon, chopped
1 onion, chopped
2 cups water
Salt and pepper, to taste
1 cup vegetable oil

Combine all ingredients except oil, mixing for 1 minute. Gradually incorporate oil, while continuing to blend. Chill.

September 5, 2001

The Umeboshi Dressing served at Sansei Seafood Restaurant & Sushi Bar can be an attention-getter over and above the actual salad it is served on.

Chef Sean Kinoshita says the dressing—made with ume, or Japanese pickled plum—has been on the Sansei menu since before the restaurant expanded from Maui to O'ahu.

It's served with mixed greens, but Kinoshita recommends serving it with a Thai grilled beef salad or as a drizzle over grilled fish. At home he uses it as a dip with simple wedges of iceberg lettuce, sliced tomatoes and cucumbers. "It's awesome: instead of a fork, I just use my hands. Tastes good that way."

Sansei Umeboshi Dressing
Makes about 4½ cups

- ¾ cup ume
- ½ cup liquid from ume jar
- 1½ cup rice vinegar
- ¾ cup sugar
- 3½ tablespoons hondashi
- 3½ tablespoons finely chopped Maui onion
- 2 teaspoons finely ground white pepper
- 3½ tablespoons soy sauce
- ¾ tablespoon dry mustard
- ¾ tablespoon chopped garlic
- 2¼ cups cottonseed oil

Remove seeds from ume and mash, to make ½ cup plus 2 tablespoons of ume paste. (**NOTE:** If your jar of ume doesn't yield ½ cup of liquid, place seeds in small amount of water and rub with the back of a spoon to release juice. Discard seeds and use flavored water to supplement liquid from the jar.)

Combine ume paste, ume liquid and all the other ingredients except the oil. Purée in blender. Drizzle in oil and continue blending until emulsified.

Dips 'n' Dressings « 85

Carbo Loading

If you're on the Atkins Diet, this is not the chapter for you. It's all about rice and noodles, local style. This is Hawai'i, where we eat rice for breakfast, and proudly. Where our plate lunches are served with double-starch, and proudly.

Yes, rice is nice. And noodles are ... fun. Both are wildly versatile. Let them lead the way.

September 5, 2007

I thought I knew all there was to know about cooking rice—rice pot, stovetop, even microwave.

Then came my conversation with Randy Manuel, executive chef at the Chart House. We were talking about fried rice, and he was saying that his customers didn't want theirs made with leftover rice.

"They don't like the rice from yesterday," is how Manuel put it.

Now, I've always thought the whole point of fried rice—the reason for its existence on Earth—is to use up leftovers. Not just rice, but leftover meat and odd veggies. Besides which, the best fried rice is made with rice that's a bit dried out, which is what happens when it sits in the fridge overnight. Some chefs even freeze their rice to get the texture right.

To use freshly made rice is to risk a mushy result.

But what are you going to do? "Some customers ask, 'Can I have the fried rice, but made with rice from today?'" Manuel said. "So we started doing it that way."

His solution is to dry-cook his rice. Instead of the normal rice-pot ratio of 1 cup rice to 1 cup water, he uses 1 cup rice to $3/4$ cup water. Clever.

Chart House Fried Rice
Serves 4

2 eggs
$1/4$ cup diced bacon
$1/4$ cup diced onion
$1/4$ cup diced carrots (see notes)
$1/4$ cup diced char siu
$1/4$ cup diced green onion
$1/2$ cup won bok kim chee
1 teaspoon hon dashi powder
1 tablespoon oyster sauce
5 cups cooked rice, warm (see notes)

Scramble egg, set aside.

Sauté bacon in skillet or wok over medium-high heat until partly cooked. Add onion; sauté until onions are soft. Add remaining ingredients, including egg. Toss until well-mixed and everything is warm.

NOTES: To soften carrots before adding to fried rice, place diced carrots in a microwave-safe dish with a small amount of water; cover and microwave on high about 30 seconds. Drain well. If using fresh rice, make rice with less water: 1 cup rice to $3/4$ cup water.

May 4, 2005

If you're in the mood for the ease of a one-dish meal, consider Bara Sushi, a sort of rice-slash-salad dish, Japanese style.

These two come courtesy of the state of Hawai'i's Department of Health, through its Start.Living.Healthy public education campaign. You'll remember the slogan from the commercial showing a guy wiping the mayonnaise off of his sandwich onto his friend's shirt (he's starting to live healthy, get it?).

Sushi can be a deceptive eating choice, seeming healthy but sometimes booby-trapped with sodium, sugar and/or fat (there's lots of mayonnaise in those dynamite rolls). And when it comes to food prep, traditional sushi can be time-consuming.

These rice mixes are packed with vegetables (and fruits in the second case). They harbor no cholesterol and little fat (none in the first case). They do, however, use white rice, not the best choice in the carbohydrate line, so if that's a serious concern, switch to brown.

The seasoning is pretty much what you'd get in standard sushi, but when it comes to preparation, it's just a matter of tossing the ingredients together. It's sushi you can eat with a fork.

Bara Sushi
Serves 8

4 cups cooked white rice
¼ cup grated carrots
½ cup french-cut beans
1½ ounces dried shiitake mushrooms, sliced

» **Sushi seasoning:**
¼ cup vinegar
¼ cup sugar
½ teaspoon salt

Mix seasoning ingredients and stir to dissolve sugar. Mix with hot rice; set aside to cool.

Steam carrots, beans and mushrooms until tender. Add to rice.

5 A Day Sushi
Serves 4

2 cups cooked rice
1 Japanese cucumber
$^1/_2$ ripe avocado, peeled
1 medium tomato
1 orange, peeled
1 papaya, peeled
1 small can mushrooms, drained
10 pitted olives
$^1/_2$ cup cooked green peas

» Rice seasoning:
5 tablespoons rice vinegar
2 tablespoons sugar

Combine rice seasoning ingredients and stir to dissolve sugar. Stir into hot rice in a bowl. Cool.

Cut cucumber, avocado, tomato, orange and papaya into $^1/_2$-inch cubes. Cut mushrooms and olives in half.

Lightly toss all the vegetables and fruits with rice mixture.

Carbo Loading « 89

November 11, 2009

Fried saimin is the Hawai'i cousin of Japanese yakisoba, and a second cousin once removed of Chinese chow mein.

All these dishes involve stir-frying noodles in a toss-up with vegetables, sliced meats, seasonings and a bit of oil. They are quick, weeknight meals of eminent flexibility: Use whatever veggies or proteins you have on hand. As with fried rice, the recipe is a moving target. Familiarize yourself with the seasonings and the basic cooking technique, buy the right noodles—the rest is up to you.

To make good fried saimin, start, of course, with good saimin noodles. This basically means the made-in-Hawai'i brands S&S (normally sold frozen) and Sun Noodle (fresh), both of which come with their own packets of dry seasoning. You use those seasoning packets to flavor the dish. This might seem like cheating and like I'm not really giving you a recipe, but if it tastes good, fills you up and makes for wholesome eating (use plenty of vegetables), why argue?

Now, if you live in a part of the world where saimin noodles aren't easy to find, substitute 1 pound chow mein noodles, preferably fresh, and use a mix of 1 tablespoon soy sauce and 1 tablespoon oyster sauce to replace the packaged seasonings.

Stir-Fried Saimin

Serves 8

5 4¹/₂ ounce packages fresh or frozen saimin noodles
Seasoning packets from saimin
2 tablespoons vegetable oil
2 teaspoons grated ginger
2 cloves garlic, minced
1 medium carrot, cut in thin strips
2 stalks celery, cut in thin strips
1 medium onion, thinly sliced
1 8-ounce package bean sprouts
4 large dried shiitake mushrooms, soaked in hot water, squeezed dry
   and thinly sliced
2 tablespoons sesame oil
1 cup thinly sliced char siu (see note)
Sliced green onion, for garnish

Add noodles to pot of boiling water, stirring for about 30 seconds to separate the strands. Do not let water return to boil. Drain well. Reserve seasoning packets.

Place vegetable oil in wok or large skillet over medium-high heat. Add ginger, garlic, carrot and celery. Stir-fry about 2 minutes, then sprinkle with contents of 1 seasoning packet. Toss.

Add onion and another seasoning packet. Stir-fry 2 more minutes. Add bean sprouts and mushrooms, plus a third seasoning packet. Stir-fry until well mixed. Remove vegetables to a serving platter.

Heat sesame oil in pan. Add noodles and sprinkle with contents of 1 or both of the remaining seasoning packets. Toss well. Add vegetables in batches to noodles, tossing to mix between additions. Turn everything onto serving platter. Top with char siu and green onion.

NOTE: Other sliced meats may be substituted for char siu, such as thinly sliced SPAM®, ham, kamaboko (Japanese fish cake) or any combination. If using SPAM®, cook along with carrots at the beginning of the process.

Carbo Loading   91

June 24, 2009

The best time to make today's recipe is right after you've had a nice Chinese dinner, provided you ordered roast duck and provided you were able to collect all the bones off everyone's plates.

The dish is Gai See Mein—sometimes spelled Kai See Mein—a noodle dish made with shredded chicken, bamboo shoots, and mushrooms, although it may be dressed up with other veggies, shredded pork, and/or ham and/or shrimp.

The goodness is in the gravy, though, and for that, you need duck bones.

I tried many cookbooks and other sources looking for the right version of this dish, and when all those failed I turned to my best source in the world of Hawai'i-style Chinese cooking, June Tong, author of the 1989 cookbook *Popo's Kitchen*.

Tong remembers the dish being a specialty of Lau Yee Chai and popular at many restaurants a generation ago. She took a day to think about it, then called back with a recipe reconstructed from memories of her family's version of the dish.

Tong says you can use any type of cooked chicken—a supermarket rotisserie bird is fine, or leftovers from KFC. The key is the gravy with its base of duck bones simmered in chicken broth. This is how she makes all her chow mein dishes. "If the gravy is good," she says, "you know the noodles will be good."

Gai See Mein

$^1/_4$ cup vegetable oil
2 pounds Hong Kong chow mein noodles
$1^1/_2$ cups shredded cooked chicken
1 cup slivered ham
Diced green onion and cilantro leaves, for garnish

» **Vegetables:**
2 tablespoons vegetable oil
1 small onion, sliced
2 stalks celery, sliced
1 carrot, peeled and sliced
$^1/_2$ pound string beans
1 8-ounce can bamboo shoot strips
1 10-ounce bag bean sprouts
Pinch salt

» **Gravy:**
2 14-ounce cans chicken broth
Bones from $^1/_2$ roast duck
1 cup shiitake mushrooms, soaked in hot water, squeezed dry and slivered
Salt, to taste
1 tablespoon oyster sauce
$^1/_4$ cup cornstarch dissolved in $^1/_4$ cup water

TO MAKE GRAVY: Bring broth to boil. Add duck bones, mushrooms, salt and oyster sauce. Simmer 15 to 20 minutes. Remove bones. Thicken with cornstarch mixture.

TO PREPARE NOODLES: Heat oil in wok or skillet. Pan-fry noodles until slightly crisp. Remove noodles.

TO PREPARE VEGETABLES: Heat oil in same wok. Stir-fry vegetables until tender-crisp, adding bean sprouts last. Season with pinch of salt.

Combine noodles, vegetables, chicken and ham. Pour hot broth over all. Garnish with green onions and cilantro.

Carbo Loading « 93

July 8, 2008

A big bowl of colored rice sits on every party table on Guam, an island that truly does know how to party. Barbecue is standard—chicken, ribs, often steak and fish—plus loads of side dishes and desserts.

It's all smoky, salty, tangy, and chili-peppery. And the canvas on which all these flavors play out is red rice.

Red rice is actually more orange, the color coming from achiote—also called achote, achuete and annatto. It's a tiny red seed familiar in Latin and Filipino cooking. Although it looks fiery—and so does the resulting rice—the flavor is mild and not at all spicy.

This recipe comes from my mother-in-law, Beatrice Calvo Perez, who makes the best red rice in the family. She relies on the finger method of measuring the water in a rice cooker, a technique used in Hawai'i and Asia (note the instructions at right). It works with any size finger, by water displacement, or perhaps magic.

Guamanian Red Rice
Serves 12

4 cups uncooked rice (preferably a mix of long- and short-grain)
1 medium onion, chopped
2 cloves garlic, minced
2 tablespoons vegetable oil
2 (14.5-ounce) cans chicken broth
2 packages ($1/3$ ounce each) achiote powder (see note)
2-ounce jar pimentos, optional, with liquid
Salt and pepper, to taste

Put all ingredients in an 8-cup rice cooker. Insert index finger straight down so it's touching the surface of the rice. Add water so that liquid reaches first joint of index finger (about 2 cups). Stir.

Start rice cooker. Halfway through cycle, stir rice.

NOTE: Achiote powder is sold in small packets in the Asian sections of many supermarkets near the seasoning packets for Filipino foods.

Microwave instructions:
Use a microwave-safe 2-quart measuring cup and make half the recipe.

Place rice in measuring cup. Rinse and drain. Sauté onions and garlic in oil. Stir into rice. Add remaining ingredients; mix. Follow the finger method of measuring (above), adding more water if necessary. Mircrowave uncovered on high 10 minutes. Stir and return to microwave for 10 more minutes. Stir and let sit a few minutes to settle.

May 23, 2001

It's rice—no, it's noodles—no, it's slippery and slimy, like ... Jell-O pasta. Long rice is one of those enigma foods. Colorless, almost tasteless, but with a distinctive texture that lends itself well to several preparations. It can be soupy, as in chicken long rice, or more solid, as in a stir-fry. It can be fried crisp or given the salad treatment in a cool, vinegary namasu.

But the request I receive most frequently is for the Japanese approach to long rice, in the style of what's dished up at an okazuya, or Japanese deli. This means it shouldn't be soupy.

The key flavors comes from soy sauce and brown sugar, mixed in small amounts with the noodles. Mix in any combination meats you have on hand. The shiitake mushrooms are important, though, if it's that okazuya version you're after.

Long Rice Special
Serves 6

- 2 bundles (about 4 ounces total) long rice
- 1/2 cup thin strips chicken
- 1/2 cup thin strips ham or luncheon meat
- 3 to 4 dried shiitake mushrooms, soaked and sliced thin
- 1 small onion, sliced
- 1/2 teaspoon grated fresh ginger
- 2 tablespoons soy sauce
- 1/4 teaspoon salt
- 1/2 teaspoon brown sugar
- 4 eggs, beaten, fried and sliced in small strips

Place long rice in cold water and bring to a boil. Drain well and cut into 2-inch lengths.

Stir-fry chicken, ham, mushrooms, onion and ginger. Add soy sauce, salt, sugar and long rice, toss to coat. Top with egg.

September 16, 2009

We have been spoiled by our rice cookers. Add rice and water, push button, walk away. It's so easy that we've forgotten how to make rice any other way—if we ever even knew. When the rice pot breaks, or we're in a place that doesn't have one, we think we can't have rice.

There are other easy ways, however, and by that I don't mean the slow simmering of rice on the stovetop. That method requires some experience and a watchful eye to prevent boil-over or burning.

But there's another heat-producing element in your kitchen—the oven—and it, too, can cook rice.

Why the oven? Because with a large enough pan you can cook rice for a crowd. It's much simpler than making two or three batches in your rice cooker, washing it out between each one. Or, if you're using the oven anyway, to roast a chicken or something, cook a cup of rice alongside it in a casserole dish—saves energy.

I've been practicing, and here's how it works, to make rice for about 25 people.

Rice for a Crowd

- **SUPPLIES:** An 8-quart aluminum roasting pan (the size normally used to keep food warm over Sterno heaters), foil and your oven.

- **INGREDIENTS:** 8 cups raw rice (white, brown, mixed, long-grain, short-grain, whatever) and boiling water. For white rice you'll need $1^1/_2$ cups water per cup of rice, so in this case, 12 cups. For brown rice the ratio is 2-to-1. For other types use slightly more water than the package recommends.

- **PROCESS:** Preheat oven to 350 degrees. Spread rice in pan (it's easiest if you don't wash the rice first, but if you can't stand that idea, be sure to drain it well). Carefully pour boiling water over rice. Stir and try to smooth rice into an even layer. Cover tightly with foil, sealing edges. Place in oven about 25 minutes for white rice, up to 45 for brown. Don't lift the foil while rice is cooking. To check for doneness, move the pan; if liquid is still sloshing around, it's not done.

- **FINISHING:** Remove pan from oven and let sit 5 to 10 minutes (if you can't stand the suspense, lift a corner and take a peek, but seal it back up). Remove foil to reveal a perfect pan of rice. Stir to fluff it up.

You'll find that the cooked rice fills about half the pan, which means you could actually cook more. Or you could cook less, using a pot—then you could boil the water and cook the rice in the same vessel. They key is to remember the water has to be boiling and the pan has to be well sealed.

March 4, 2009

My rice cooker broke a few years ago and I've never replaced it. It's not that we don't eat rice, I've just figured out how to make it without keeping another small appliance on the counter.

I use a 2-quart Pyrex glass measuring cup and the microwave, a technique I learned from Carole Mito in a microwave cooking class she taught in 2003.

When I tell people about this, their eyes light up as though I have just explained magic. Some have immediately gone out to buy the measuring cup. It struck me that if I put this in writing, more people might find me magical.

Microwave Rice

So here's what you do: combine 3 cups white rice and 3 cups water in a 2-quart (8-cup) microwave-safe container. Or use the knuckle method of measuring the water (insert pointer finger straight through water, touching top of rice; water level should reach first knuckle).

Microwave, uncovered, on high, 15 to 20 minutes. In my microwave, it takes exactly 18 minutes. The rice is done when all the water is absorbed. There might be a bit of scum on top, but do not be alarmed. Just stir well and let it sit a few minutes.

This method works for brown rice or hapa rice (mixed white and brown), but the cooking time will be as much as 25 minutes and you have to add more water. You can make 1 to 3 cups of rice this way. Don't try to get away with a smaller cooking container, though, or you'll have boil-over even when you're starting with only a cup of rice.

I cook rice this way when using packaged mixes for rice pilaf and such, too.

You don't really save time with this method, but it means you don't have to have the extra appliance, and cleanup is a bit simpler. If you have leftovers, you can put the whole container in the fridge and put it back in the microwave the next day.

The Main Event

If you think of dinner as a stage production, the main dish is the diva. Perhaps other elements are crucial–rice for support, salad for fluff and color–but the entrée sells the tickets.

To further strain the metaphor, the main dish is the star of the show. You, as director of this production, cast the part based on what inspires you at the market, or perhaps what you've got stashed away in the freezer. This is where dinner begins.

On with the show.

May 10, 2000

The Angelo Pietro restaurant chain was founded in Japan in 1980 based on a marriage of classic Italian dishes and Japanese flavor bases.

On Pietro menus you'll find spaghetti in a salad, cold with a soy-based dressing or sesame-miso sauce. A mushroom pasta is made with shiitake and enoki mushrooms, with a cream or soy-based sauce. Clam Pepperoncini is poached in white wine, spicy soy sauce, and garlic.

This popular chicken dish includes the Japanese seasonings of soy sauce and hondashi (fish stock).

Angelo Pietro Chicken and Spinach Spaghetti

Serves 4

3 skinless, boneless chicken breasts, cut in 1-by-1-inch pieces
2 tablespoons soy sauce
2 heaping tablespoons flour
2 tablespoons vegetable oil
6 ounces spinach leaves
1 pound spaghetti (Barilla No. 5 preferred), cooked

» Chicken seasoning:
$1/2$ tablespoon garlic purée
$1/2$ teaspoon white pepper
$1/2$ teaspoon salt
Pinch chili-pepper flakes, crushed

» Sauté pan seasoning:
Dash garlic purée
Pinch salt
2 tablespoons hondashi fish stock
Splash soy sauce

» Garlic-oil sauce:
1 cup vegetable oil
$1/3$ cup sliced raw garlic
1 tablespoon crushed dried chili-pepper flakes

TO PREPARE CHICKEN: Lightly coat with soy sauce, then lightly season with chicken-seasoning ingredients. Lightly dust with flour.

Heat 2 tablespoons oil and brown chicken. Stir in spinach just until wilted. Add sauté pan seasonings (sauce should be a dark tan color and not too thick).

TO PREPARE GARLIC-OIL SAUCE: Sauté oil and garlic on high heat until garlic is golden brown. With a slotted spoon, remove garlic. Let oil and garlic cool, then return garlic chips to oil and add chili flakes.

Toss pasta with chicken mixture and garlic-oil sauce.

The Main Event « 101

March 13, 2002

If you went to public school in Hawai'i and ate in the cafeteria, this dish will be quite familiar. If you have kids at the elementary school level, this may well be among their favorite dishes, even if they haven't verbalized the thought.

When I was in school it was called baked spaghetti—the pasta and sauce all familiar, but the form somehow more solid.

This is the version served at Lunalilo Elementary School, where cook Reagan Tyau says the dish pops up every five weeks on the menu and is a favorite of the kids.

The secret appears to be the addition of quite a bit of American cheese, which boosts the protein content of the dish. "Kids just love cheese in general," Tyau says.

Once cooked, the sauce is mixed in with the cooked pasta and the pans are put under 200-degree warmers and held until lunchtime. Tyau says the noodles absorb a lot of the sauce, making the dish quite firm—in fact, you can cut it like lasagna. (Interesting contradiction: the kids don't much care for lasagna, Tyau says.) To recreate this effect at home, place your pan in a warm oven.

The recipe that follows was cut down from Lunalilo's hundred-portion formula. I tried it out at home, where the reception was inversely proportional to age: The kindergartner was quite happy; the sixteen-year-old said, "School food??!!" and accused me of trying to kill him.

Depending on how saucy you like your pasta, you might want to play around with the amount of noodles you fix. The school's original recipe seemed to offer a lot of pasta to sauce. This recipe cuts the proportion somewhat. Also, to suit adult tastes, the amount of cheese could be cut in half.

Lunalilo School Spaghetti
Serves 10

1 pound ground beef
3 tablespoons dehydrated onions
2 (1¹/₂ ounce) packages spaghetti sauce mix (McCormick brand preferred)
Pepper to taste
¹/₂ teaspoon dried oregano
1 teaspoon granulated garlic
5 cups crushed tomatoes
1¹/₂ tablespoons chicken base (see note)
¹/₂ to 1 teaspoon Worcestershire sauce
³/₄ teaspoon sugar, or more to taste
Salt to taste
10 ounces American cheese (13 slices)
1 pound uncooked spaghetti

Brown ground beef. Drain fat; add onions, spaghetti sauce mix, pepper, oregano and garlic. Stir in tomatoes, chicken base, Worcestershire, sugar and salt. Bring to a boil; reduce heat and simmer 45 minutes.

Meanwhile cook spaghetti. Drain, but do not rinse.

Stir cheese into sauce to melt, then stir in spaghetti.

Transfer pasta and sauce to a baking pan and cover with foil. Place in a 200-degree oven for 1 hour.

NOTE: Chicken base is a paste, sold in supermarkets alongside chicken broth or boullion.

The Main Event « 103

March 17, 2004

L et's say fifty Boy Scouts are coming to dinner and you were only planning on forty. Time to stretch. Some suggestions from a master:

- If you're making spaghetti, let the noodles overcook. Fattened with water, they'll expand: suddenly, more spaghetti!

- If you're making hamburgers, add lots of bread to the ground beef. "If you have enough flavor in there, people don't notice you got lots of bread in there."

That's advice born of experience from Herb Yasukochi, longtime Scout master for the Honpa Hongwanji Hawai'i Betsuin. He's accustomed to taking fifty or sixty boys on weeklong summer camps, during which bulk cooking is the order of the day.

OK, so spaghetti with overly fat noodles won't please a gourmand, but how many of those go camping with the Boy Scouts? "When you're at the beach, you're hungry, you eat anything," Yasukochi says. "I was surprised how much the boys like spaghetti."

But for the annual Taste of Hongwanji bazaar, Yasukochi makes beef stew that has not been artificially stretched, using a proven recipe that begins with beef chuck, short ribs and Portuguese sausage.

Yasukochi, a service manager for The Gas Co., has been involved with the Scouts since childhood, serving as a leader since his sons joined the temple troop twenty-one years ago.

He also leads cooking classes for Scouts. Boys are enthusiastic about cooking, he says, if it means they get to eat well. The results are surprising to parents. "They'll say, 'Mr. Y, you know what happened? You taught my boy to cook, so we had stir-fry all weekend.' "

Herb's Scout Stew
Serves 20

- 2 pounds beef chuck roast, cubed
- 1 pound boneless beef short ribs, in bite-sized pieces
- 6 cloves garlic, smashed
- 1/4 cup vegetable oil, divided
- 2 teaspoons chicken base (see note)
- 2 teaspoons beef base (see note)
- 2 15-ounce cans tomato sauce
- 1 6-ounce can tomato paste
- 1 3-inch piece ginger, peeled and sliced
- 4 bay leaves
- 1 pound carrots, sliced
- 6 medium potatoes, cubed
- 6 onions, chopped
- 6 stalks celery, sliced
- 1 tablespoon Hawaiian salt
- 12 ounces Portuguese sausage, sliced
- 1 11-ounce can corn
- 1/2 cup soy sauce
- 2 tablespoons flour
- 1/4 cup water

Brown beef, ribs and garlic in half of the oil in a stock pot. Add chicken and beef base, tomato sauce, tomato paste, ginger and bay leaves to pot. Add water to cover ingredients. Simmer 1 hour over medium-high heat, until meat is tender.

Brown carrots, potatoes, onions and celery in remaining oil in a wok or skillet. Season with Hawaiian salt. Add vegetables, sausage and corn to pot and simmer another 30 minutes.

Combine soy sauce, flour and water; stir until smooth. Add to pot to thicken. Taste and adjust seasonings with more salt if necessary.

NOTE: Chicken and beef base are paste-like soup concentrates. They are sold in supermarkets near the bouillons and stocks.

The Main Event

April 28, 2004

This is the circle of life here at recipe central: readers eat divine dishes at restaurants, dream of recreating them at home, then ask for the recipes. We ask the appropriate chefs. Often they say yes; sometimes they say no, and sometimes they offer a compromise. Such is the case today.

Alan Takasaki, chef at Le Bistro, says the recipe for Barbecued Lamb Chops is one he'd rather not give out, as the dish is among the top sellers at his restaurant. He did, however, take the time to come up with a grilled lamb chop recipe that he says is similar in flavor and more practical for cooking at home.

Takasaki guesses that his dish has caught on because it's different. Lamb served around town is generally made with hoisin, that pungent Chinese sauce made of soy beans and chili peppers. Takasaki uses red wine, balsamic vinegar and honey, plus lots of herbs in his marinade, then serves his finished chops with a red wine sauce.

The dish does take a little time and a lot of different ingredients, mainly in the form of fresh and dried herbs. But Takasaki says it is not tricky. The only thing to remember is not to overcook it on the grill; it'll blacken quickly.

Barbecued Lamb Chops

Serves 5

10 lamb chops

» Marinade:
  $1/4$ cup EACH chopped shallots, garlic and fennel
  $1/4$ cup extra-virgin olive oil
  $1/2$ cup red wine
  1 teaspoon EACH fresh thyme leaves, rosemary leaves and chopped mint
  2 teaspoons EACH chopped Italian parsley and tube chives
  $1/4$ teaspoon EACH cracked black pepper and Herbs de Provence
  1 cup EACH balsamic vinegar and honey

» Red Wine Sauce:
  1 tablespoon shallots
  1 teaspoon fresh thyme leaves
  1 teaspoon butter
  1 cup EACH balsamic vinegar, honey and red wine
  1 cup veal stock

TO MAKE MARINADE: Sauté shallots, garlic and fennel in oil. Add wine and simmer until reduced to a syrup. Add other herbs. Stir in honey and vinegar. Pour over chops and marinate in refrigerator 2 hours.

Grill chops until medium rare, about 3 minutes per side. Chops may also be cooked in a frying pan.

TO MAKE SAUCE: Sauté shallots and thyme in butter, then add vinegar, honey and red wine. Reduce to a syrup and add veal stock. Reduce by half. Serve with lamb chops.

NOTES: Tube chives have rounded stems, not flat stems like garlic chives. Herbs de Provence is a combination of dried herbs such as marjoram, thyme, savory, basil, rosemary, sage and fennel seeds.

April 18, 2001

Maria Whitt comes to restaurant ownership from the unlikely profession of landscaping, with no cooking school background. She is, however, from the School of Why Not? and so when the opportunity to take over a small restaurant near Diamond Head came up, she went for it. "I've always been a frustrated chef," Whitt says.

She has been running Bogart's Cafe on Monsarrat Avenue for six months, serving espresso along with omelets, pancakes and her top seller, a bagel with egg, cheese, tomato and spinach. Later in the day, she offers sandwiches and lunch specials.

One of these is a shrimp and pasta dish with sun-dried tomatoes and pesto. Whitt says she threw the dish together one day using things available in the kitchen when she needed a meal in a hurry. "It can be done in five minutes."

Bogart's Shrimp Pasta with Sun-Dried Tomatoes
Serves 4

1 pound penne rigatoni
1 pound large shrimp, peeled
$1/4$ cup olive oil
$1/2$ cup sun-dried tomatoes packed in oil
2 tablespoons pesto
2 teaspoons minced garlic
1 cup portobello mushrooms, sliced and sautéed
$1/2$ cup Parmesan cheese
Salt and pepper to taste

Prepare pasta according to package directions. While it is cooking, prepare sauce: Sauté shrimp in olive oil. When nearly done, add remaining ingredients and toss to mix. Drain pasta and toss with sauce.

November 19, 2008

Thanksgiving (eight more days!) is a day for thinking big: big bird, big dinner. Some celebrations are small, though, and for those, here's an alternative to a whole roasted turkey.

If you don't need it for Thanksgiving, it's also a good recipe to keep in your back pocket for the frenzy-packed days leading up to ... what was that other holiday? Oh yeah: Christmas.

The dish is called Coca-Cola Turkey, and it's served at The Alley Restaurant at Aiea Bowl. Chef Shane Masutani uses strips of breast meat that are marinated in a teriyaki-like mix of soy sauce, garlic and ginger, but with Coke and Sprite instead of sugar. At the restaurant, the meat is grilled and served in sandwiches and salads.

If it's too much trouble to break out the hibachi, Masutani suggests using a grill pan on the stove. Pan-frying will also work, but should be a last resort, he said. "Grilling adds a different dimension to the turkey with bits of charred turkey on the outside while remaining tender and moist."

I tested this recipe using chicken breast tenders (the supermarket only had whole, solidly frozen turkeys, no pieces), using a grill pan on a portable gas burner. It got rave reviews from the family. In fact, I hardly got to eat any of it.

Alley Restaurant Coca-Cola Turkey
Serves 2

1 pound turkey breast meat, cut into strips

» Marinade:
1 cup Coca-Cola
1 cup Sprite
6 tablespoons soy sauce
2 teaspoons minced garlic
1 teaspoon minced ginger
$1/_2$ teaspoon fresh cracked pepper
$1/_2$ cup vegetable oil

Combine marinade ingredients and pour over turkey. Marinate, refrigerated, at least 4 hours.

Prepare a charcoal or gas grill.

Remove turkey from marinade and grill over medium heat until cooked through, but not overcooked or it will be dry. Let rest a few minutes.

August 6, 2008

A Cornish game hen is a small young chicken, typically less than 2 pounds and about 5 weeks old. The hens are easy to find frozen, and their size makes them ideal for dinners for one or two.

They're also a favorite of slow-cooker meals, as three or four fit easily inside the typical Crock-Pot. Most recipes, though, call for oven-roasting, which nicely browns them all around.

But I was looking for a pot-roast-type recipe for stove-top cooking, a method that would be quicker than the oven or slow cooker. Those are rare, but I came across one developed by Tyson Foods. It called for a mix of herbs and a bit of white wine that combine to simmer subtle flavor into the hens.

I tested it with fresh thyme and rosemary, and used vermouth, a fortified wine, diluted with water. You could play with the flavors by using another combination of herbs, or using wine (red or white), beer, sake or even cider. The dish yields a very flavorful broth that can be thickened into a light gravy.

One thing about Cornish hens: They leave you with quite a bit of fat. If you have the time to refrigerate the juices overnight, you'll be able to scoop off a half-cup of solidified fat. If you don't have the time, skim as much fat as you can from the juices or you'll taste the greasiness.

Cornish Hen Pot Roast

Serves 4

2 Cornish game hens (about 22 ounces each)
1 teaspoons dry thyme, or 1 tablespoon fresh leaves
1 teaspoon dry rosemary, or 1 tablespoon fresh, minced
1 clove garlic, minced
1 teaspoon salt
Pinch pepper
2 tablespoons olive oil
$^1/_2$ cup vermouth (see note)
$^1/_2$ cup water
1 tablespoon cornstarch, dissolved in $^1/_4$ cup warm water

Rinse hens with cold water and pat dry with paper towels. Split hens in half by cutting down backbone, then through breastbone.

Combine herbs, garlic, salt and pepper. Rub mixture over both sides of hens.

Heat oil in Dutch oven over medium-high heat. Brown hens well on all sides.

Add vermouth; reduce heat. Cover and simmer 45 minutes, until juices run clear when thigh is pierced with a fork. Remove hens; cover.

Strain juices in pot and skim fat (there will be a lot; if possible refrigerate to let fat solidify). Bring to juices simmer and stir in cornstarch mixture. Stir until slightly thickened. Serve sauce with hens.

NOTE: A dry white wine may be used in place of vermouth. Use a full cup and eliminate water.

The Main Event « 111

August 23, 2000

When Ram Arora agreed to share his curry recipe, there was a catch. Arora flavors his curry with a masala mix prepared for him at his family's restaurant in New Delhi. It's made of twenty to twenty-five spices—among them cloves, cinnamon and cardamom—that are dried whole in the sun, then ground. "A lot of labor and time are involved," Arora says.

Masala spice mixes are available at specialty cooking stores and health food markets, but the chances that you'll hit on the Arora family's precise mix are slim. Follow this recipe, though, and you could get close to the intensely flavored curry served at the restaurant on South King Street.

Just keep in mind that good curry is dependent on good spices, Arora says, so seek out the freshest and the best.

He also offers this tip in the way of technique: His curry is finished at low heat, after a quick combining of all the ingredients in a hot pan. "If you cook at low heat the natural juice comes out and that's where the good taste is."

India House Chicken Curry
Serves 4

1/2 teaspoon turmeric
2 to 3 tablespoons masala spice mix
Salt and red chili powder to taste
1/2 cup vegetable oil
2 large onions, sliced lengthwise
2 tablespoons yogurt
2 small sticks cinnamon
2 to 3 bay leaves
3 to 4 cardamom seeds
Pinch ground ginger
5 to 6 cloves garlic, smashed and minced
1 4-pound chicken, skinned, boned and cut in bite-sized pieces

Combine turmeric, masala, salt and chili powder to make a paste. Set aside.

Heat the oil in a wok and fry onions until light brown. Stir in yogurt, cinnamon, bay leaves, cardamoms, ginger and garlic. Cook until onions are completely brown.

Add chicken and enough water to partially cover. Bring to a boil and add masala mix. Reduce heat to low; cover and cook until chicken is done. Stir occasionally so mixture doesn't stick.

September 17, 2008

Never accuse Eddie Flores of thinking small. Not only has he taken the local grinds of his L&L Drive-Inns nationwide, but now he's planning to invade mainland supermarkets with L&L's Barbecued Chicken.

The chicken will be sold frozen in 2.5-pound boxes, pre-marinated and ready to defrost and cook. To be certain the product is user-friendly, Flores had his marketing director, Brandon Dela Cruz, cook up a batch. "You gotta have the regular guy who doesn't know how to cook," he said. "You think it's funny, but that's how you test the food, right?"

Flores said the chicken is L&L's top seller along with Chicken Katsu. His executive chef, Raymond Cheng, says the recipe is thirty years old. The chicken is one of the dishes that helped launch the company, he says. "That's how we came up."

L&L Drive-Inn Barbecued Chicken

4 pounds chicken thighs, deboned, skin on

» **Marinade:**
3 cups soy sauce
1 cup sugar
1 cup water
½ teaspoon minced ginger
¼ teaspoon minced garlic
¼ teaspoon black pepper

BUTTERFLY CHICKEN: After removing the bone, place thigh on cutting board and spread it apart so it lies flat. If necessary, cut through side of the thigh, holding knife parallel to cutting board, slicing almost but not all the way through. Spread the halves apart and flatten.

Combine marinade ingredients and add chicken. Marinate, refrigerated, 4 to 5 hours.

Chicken may be pan-fried, grilled over charcoal or baked at 350 degrees for about 20 minutes. (At L&L, the chicken is cooked on the restaurants' griddles.)

Sept. 15, 1999

Helen Bajo, a veteran laulau maker, says there are very few rules for making laulau. "Laulau could be anything. The variety could be endless—just use your imagination."

Try Samoan-themed chicken with coconut milk and onions, or corned beef with cabbage and carrots.

Good ingredients, Bajo says, include half-ripe breadfruit, pumpkin, sweet potato, carrots and other hard root vegetables. Softer vegetables such as tomatoes can be used with pre-cooked meat or in seafood or vegetarian bundles that have shorter cooking times. They will disintegrate and their flavors intensify, so use lightly. Onions should be cut in big chunks or they will disappear.

And remember, laulau must include some fat and salt. The traditional pork laulau is one-third fat, with a cube of salted butterfish or salmon for moisture and taste. When using chicken, use the fatter thighs; with lower fat or vegetarian combinations, compensate with coconut chunks or coconut milk.

These recipes are from Bajo's son, Kalei, who explains that he puts his laulau in a pot with water and then turns on the stove. Cooking times begin then, not when the water is boiling. Assemble several of one type of laulau or mix and match. They can all go into the pot together.

Note that these recipes are designed for a type of lū'au leaf called lehua, not the Chinese lū'au leaf that is most common in supermarkets. Chinese lū'au leaves have to be cooked longer because of their higher level of calcium oxalate crystals in the raw leaves, which produce an itch in the mouth. If all you can find is Chinese lū'au (other types are available at farmer's markets), increase cooking time or precook the leaves slightly.

Chicken and Pumpkin Laulau

$^1/_2$ cup fresh pumpkin in 1-inch squares; leave skin on
1 chicken thigh
$^1/_8$ cup dried shrimp
$^1/_4$ cup Maui onion
Pinch pepper
1 teaspoon sea salt or Hawaiian salt
4 lū'au leaves
2 ti leaves

Wrap ingredients in lū'au leaves, sprinkling some salt between the leaves. Wrap in ti leaves. Place laulau bundle in steamer over water and turn on stove. Steam 4 hours (start timer after water starts boiling).

Seafood Laulau

- 6 jumbo shrimp
- 1/4 cup bay scallops
- 1 piece calamari, in bite-sized pieces, about 2 ounces
- 1/4 cup diced Maui onion
- 1 teaspoon garlic powder
- Pinch pepper
- 1 teaspoon sea salt or Hawaiian salt
- 4 large lū'au leaves, ribs removed
- 2 large ti leaves

Mix together seafood and onion; sprinkle with spices. Wrap ingredients in lū'au leaves, sprinkling between leaves with salt. Wrap in ti leaves. Place laulau bundles in steamer over water and turn on stove. Steam 2 hours (start timer after water starts boiling).

Vegetarian Laulau

- 3 ounces sweet potato, cut in 4 pieces
- 1/8 block tofu (about 2.5 ounces)
- 1/4 cup fresh coconut in bite-sized pieces
- 1/8 cup diced Maui onion
- 2-inch square piece aburage (fried bean curd), quartered
- Pinch pepper
- 1 teaspoon sea salt or Hawaiian salt
- 4 lū'au leaves
- 2 ti leaves

Wrap all ingredients in lū'au leaf, sprinkling some salt between the luau leaves. Wrap bundle in ti leaves. Place laulau bundles in steamer over water and turn on stove. Steam 2 hours (start timer after water starts boiling).

March 13, 2002

For the last year, I have been trying to develop a meaningful relationship with my CrockPot. He has betrayed me often, though, leaving me disappointed and broken-hearted, my stews overcooked, my vegetables an unattractive shade of beige.

Some of my friends have cast their crocks out of the house, unable to deal with their unpredictability.

But I remain committed, because there is nothing better to come home to than a nice, hot meal ready to scoop out of the pot. And the only way to get this, short of a private chef or a very cooperative older child, is a Crock-Pot.

I am not interested in typical slow-cooker recipes that average five or six hours of cooking time. I want dishes that can be started when I go out the door and won't reach their peak until I get home nine or ten hours later. I want my life made easier.

So began a search, which led to this recipe merger of traditional Hawaiian with the modern cooking technique of the slow cooker. It comes from my friend Marilyn Ige.

Slow Cooker Laulau
Serves 8

3 pounds lū'au leaves
3 pounds boneless pork, in 2-inch chunks
2$^{1}/_{2}$ tablespoons Hawaiian salt
$^{3}/_{4}$ cup water

Wash lū'au leaves and remove stems and fibrous parts of veins. Bring a large pot of water to a boil and wilt leaves, boiling them about 3 minutes. Drain.

Rub pork with Hawaiian salt, kneading thoroughly.

Layer wilted lū'au leaf in crock pot with pork. Add water. Cook on low heat 9 to 10 hours, or until lū'au leaves are cooked.

March 5, 2008

The Golden Dragon roared its last on February 3. After fifty years, the Hilton Hawaiian Village's Chinese restaurant fell victim to a decline in business. Another longtime local restaurant gone, but not forgotten.

It was the Mongolian Lamb that one reader missed most—"one of the best meat dishes I've ever eaten," she said.

The dish, from Golden Dragon chef Steve Chiang, centers on strips of lamb loin marinated in a mixture rich with brandy. The lamb is quickly stir-fried, then given another dose of brandy—along with hoisin, soy sauce and sugar—in a sauce.

Golden Dragon Mongolian Lamb
Serves 2

- 6 ounces lamb loin, sliced
- 3 tablespoons vegetable oil
- 4 stalks green onion, in 2-inch pieces
- ½ piece ginger, in strips

» **Marinade:**
- 1 tablespoon cornstarch
- 1 tablespoon oil
- 1 tablespoon water
- 1 tablespoon brandy

» **Sauce:**
- 2 tablespoons soy sauce
- 1 tablespoon hoisin sauce
- 1 tablespoon brandy
- 1 tablespoon sugar
- 1 tablespoon sesame oil
- ¼ cup chicken stock
- 1 tablespoon cornstarch

Combine marinade ingredients and marinate lamb 2 hours.

TO MAKE SAUCE: Bring all ingredients to a boil, thickening with cornstarch. Set aside.

Heat wok and add vegetable oil. Add lamb and stir-fry until done. Add ginger and green onion, then add sauce.

January 20, 1999

The key to paella is saffron—"the world's most expensive spice," says Chef Fred DeAngelo of Palomino Euro Bistro. Saffron is the pistil of the purple crocus, and it takes two thousand strands to make a single ounce, DeAngelo says. He buys his by the ounce—at $40 per. "I keep it locked up in my office."

Paella is a signature dish at Palomino and among the restaurant's most popular. It has an impressive list of ingredients, from chorizo to king crab. Putting it together could be an expensive proposition—the saffron alone could break the bank. Luckily, a little spice goes a long way and this recipe calls for just $1/2$ teaspoon. You can get saffron at kitchen specialty shops and at some supermarkets.

The cooking of this classic Spanish dish has been simplified somewhat, DeAngelo said. Traditionally, you'd prepare it completely in the oven, cooking the rice until three-quarters done, then adding the seafood in parts, depending on how long each type needs to cook, returning the dish to the oven each time. He cooks the rice in the oven, then finishes it on the stove top.

Palomino Euro Bistro Paella
Serves 3

3 teaspoons olive oil
6 cloves garlic, minced
9 ounces mahimahi
9 live clams
9 live mussels
Salt and pepper to taste, about $1/4$ teaspoon each
6 ounces fish stock or clam juice
6 ounces white wine
Juice of $1^1/_2$ lemons
9 large shrimp (16-20 size)
3 king crab claws or legs, cut in half and split
3 ounces peas

» Prepared rice (Makes $2^1/_2$ cups):
1 ounce olive oil
1 link chorizo, rough cut
5 ounces chicken thigh meat, in chunks
1 medium Maui onion, $1/_2$-inch dice
$1/_2$ red pepper, $1/_2$-inch dice
$1/_2$ green pepper, $1/_2$-inch dice
2 cloves garlic, minced
2 ounces vermouth
4 roma tomatoes, $1/_2$-inch dice
$1/_2$ teaspoon dried oregano
$1/_2$ teaspoon dried thyme
$3/_4$ teaspoon coriander
1 teaspoon cumin
$1/_4$ teaspoon crushed peppers
$1/_2$ teaspoon saffron
1 cup chicken stock
$1/_2$ pound long-grain rice

TO MAKE THE RICE: Heat oil, brown chorizo and chicken. Add onions, peppers and garlic, deglaze with vermouth. Add tomatoes, spices and stock, bring to a boil. Add rice, cover and bake about $1/_2$ hour in a 375-degree oven.

TO PREPARE PAELLA: Combine oil, garlic, fish, clams and mussels and sauté over medium heat. Season with salt and pepper. Deglaze pan with stock and wine, add lemon juice, cover and reduce until shellfish open, about 1 minute.

Add shrimp, crab, rice and peas, gently stir, then cover and cook another 2 minutes. Garnish with lemon slices and chopped parsley.

NOTE: If you don't have a large enough pan to hold all the ingredients at once, divide the prepared rice and the paella ingredients into 3 equal parts and prepare one portion at a time.

The Main Event « 119

June 13, 2001

We're going to play word association. I'll give you the name of a dish and you answer with the first reaction that comes to mind.

Pig's Feet Soup.

Depending on your cultural bent, you either said, "Blech! Get away from me!" or, "Where? I want some now!"

Ashitibichi, in Okinawan, is warm, soul-satisfying, comfort food, considered health food, actually, because the gelatin that slowly cooks out of the feet and into the broth and is believed to prevent deterioration of the knee ligaments.

That gelatin, released over two or more hours of cooking, is also what gives the soup its special taste.

This recipe for the classic soup is based on one in *Okinawan Mixed Plate: Generous Servings of Culture, Customs and Cuisines*, published by Hui O Laulima, the women's auxiliary of the Hawai'i United Okinawa Association.

The original began with the traditional preparation of the pig's feet: singe by holding over the flame of a gas burner, hibachi, or electric stove coil until the skin is burnt. Scrape off burned areas and wash. Thankfully, that step is unnecessary these days, with clean pig forelegs—already cut in pieces—available frozen at supermarkets.

Ashitibichi (Pig's Feet Soup)
Serves 6 to 8

2 to 3 pounds pig's feet
5 cups water
1 thumb-sized piece ginger, sliced
2 strips nishimi kubu (see note)
6 medium dried shiitake mushrooms
2 cups daikon (turnip) chunks (or more, to taste)
$1/4$ cup soy sauce or miso
1 teaspoon Hawaiian salt
2 tablespoons sake
1 small bunch mustard cabbage, parboiled and cut in 2-inch lengths
(may substitute watercress or winter melon)

The day before, cover pig's feet in water and bring to a rolling boil; drain and rinse. Return to pot and cover with the 5 cups water. Boil 10 minutes at high heat. Reduce heat to medium for 15 minutes, then add ginger. Cook 30 minutes more until meat is tender. Refrigerate pig's feet and stock separately overnight.

The next day, remove fat from stock.

Wash kubu; tie knots about 3 inches apart. Cut into sections. Soak shiitake in warm water with pinch sugar, 20 to 30 minutes. Reserve liquid; cut mushrooms into quarters, discarding stems.

Combine reserved mushroom water with enough stock to make 7 cups. Add pig's feet, kubu, mushrooms and daikon; cook 10 minutes. Add soy or miso, salt and sake; cover and simmer 1 hour, gently stirring 2 or 3 times.

Just before serving, add mustard cabbage. Grated ginger may be served as a condiment.

NOTE: Nishimi kubu is Okinawan-style konbu, or dried kelp, prepared specially for nishimi (in Japanese, nishime; in English, vegetables stewed with a small amount of meat). It is thinner than regular konbu. Nishimi kubu is available at Japanese or Asian markets. If you can't find it, substitute regular konbu.

May 15, 2002

That triple combo of soy sauce, sugar and ginger is the basis of so many simple, reliable and familiar Japanese dishes.

This one is so basic that many home cooks carry versions around in their heads. They're great for beginners who'd like to put something on the table that speaks of home, such as one reader who wrote to me seeking a pork tofu recipe like his mother's. He remembered it having sliced pork, onions and mushrooms, as well as tofu, and so good you could eat it straight from the skillet.

So, get out the shoyu bottle and the ginger grater. If you haven't had a nice steaming dish of pork tofu in a few years, this will remind you of how savory and comforting something so simple can be.

One note: The recipe seems to call for very little liquid, but it is plenty. Enough water comes out of the tofu, even as it absorbs the sweet soy-ginger flavors, to provide lots of sauce for spooning over hot rice.

Just Like Mom's Pork Tofu
Serves 4

- ½ pound lean pork, thinly sliced
- 1 small onion, thinly sliced
- 8 to 10 stalks green onion, in 1½ inch lengths
- 2 tablespoons vegetable oil
- 1 pound tofu, drained and cubed

» Sauce:
- ¼ cup soy sauce
- 1 tablespoon mirin
- 2 tablespoons sugar
- 2 teaspoons slivered or grated fresh ginger

Combine sauce ingredients; stir to dissolve sugar and set aside.

Stir-fry pork and onions in oil until pork is nearly cooked through. Pour sauce over pork and onions and simmer 5 minutes.

Gently stir in tofu cubes so that they are well-coated with sauce and turn light brown. Spoon with lots of sauce over hot rice.

VARIATIONS: You can stir in up to 1 cup of watercress, mushrooms, bamboo shoots, beans or bell peppers without increasing the liquid in the pan.

April 5, 2000

Just luck, Seiju Ifuku says. Luck that he returned from World War II uninjured. Luck that the army taught him to cook. Luck that he and his wife, Ayako, were able to open a restaurant in Kapahulu they named Rainbow, and that it earned them a tiny pot of gold. Luck that his sons-in-law were willing to take over when the time came, so the drive-in could stay in the family.

But we all know luck had nothing to do with it.

Attribute this success to endless hours of hard work, good sense about the drive-in business—and brains.

"You gotta be lucky," Ifuku insists. "You gotta have timing. And guts. Little bit guts."

Opening day was October 2, 1961, when Rainbow Drive-In served its first plate lunch in the modest building on Kapahulu Avenue. And that's the way it's been for nearly four decades, under the Rainbow.

In a day, Rainbow Drive-In sells 900 to 1,200 plate lunches and 300 to 500 sandwiches. The menu hasn't changed much—the last time a new item was added was two years ago, roast pork. "My motto is 'Give plenty, and quick service,'" Ifuku says.

This is a half-portion of the Shoyu Chicken normally cooked up at Rainbow Drive-In, the smallest amount the cooks felt comfortable issuing without re-testing the recipe. If you reduce it further, be sure to check the flavorings.

Rainbow Drive-In Shoyu Chicken
Serves 12

12 pounds chicken thighs

» Sauce:
2 1/2 cups sugar
3 1/4 cups soy sauce
3/4 to 1 cup vinegar
1/2 teaspoon salt
1/2 teaspoon pepper
6 dashes Worcestershire sauce
3 to 4 cloves garlic, crushed
3 to 5 inches ginger, crushed

Wash and drain chicken. Combine sauce ingredients.

Combine chicken and sauce in a pot. Bring to a boil and cook until chicken is tender, 20 to 30 minutes. Skim sauce. Thicken with flour or cornstarch. Bring to a boil again and serve.

The Main Event

September 5, 2001

Just about every restaurant has a dish or two that can't be removed from the menu because the customers won't allow it. At Ryan's Grill that would be the Cajun Chicken Fettuccini.

Chef Bill Bruhl says the recipe came from Paul Prudhomme's New Orleans restaurant years ago when Prudhomme trained several Ryan's chefs on Cajun seasonings and Cajun dishes. "It's an item I would never even think of removing from the menu."

The complexity of the dish is what makes it work, Bruhl says, specifically the blend of seven dry spices rubbed into the chicken.

The restaurant makes this dish in large quantities, so portions had to be reduced to make it practical for home use. This explains some of the odd proportions (such as 1³/₄ cup plus 2 tablespoons chicken stock). Your results may be slightly different from what you've had at the restaurant, but you should be within striking distance.

Ryan's Grill Cajun Chicken Fettuccini
Serves 8

2 pounds chicken tenderloins, in 1-by-1-inch pieces
3 tablespoons Spice Blend (recipe follows)
¹/₂ pound unsalted butter
1¹/₂ pounds fettuccini, blanched al denté
Fresh grated Parmesan cheese, for garnish
Green onion curls, for garnish (see note)

» Sauce:
6 ounces (³/₄ cup) unsalted butter
¹/₃ medium onion, in ¹/₈-inch dice
3 whole garlic cloves
1¹/₂ tablespoons minced garlic
Scant 2 teaspoons thyme
1 heaping teaspoon cayenne
Scant teaspoon white pepper
Pinch black pepper
Scant ¹/₂ teaspoon dried basil
1³/₄ cups plus 2 tablespoons chicken stock
1¹/₂ tablespoons Worcestershire sauce
3 teaspoons hot sauce (such as Tabasco)
3 cups tomato sauce
1¹/₃ tablespoons sugar
¹/₃ bunch green onions, in ¹/₈-inch slices

124   » The Main Event

TO MAKE SAUCE: Melt butter over medium-high heat. Add onions and whole garlic; sauté 5 minutes. Add minced garlic and dry seasonings. Cook until onions are dark brown.

Add stock, Worcestershire and hot sauce. Bring to a rapid simmer and cook 20 minutes.

Add tomato sauce and return sauce to a simmer. Stir in sugar and green onions and continue to simmer for 1 hour.

TO PREPARE PASTA: Rub chicken pieces with Spice Blend.

Melt butter over medium heat. Add chicken and sauté until just cooked. Add sauce and cook 1 1/2 to 2 minutes. Add pasta and toss to coat. Continue to sauté until sauce clings to pasta.

Serve in large dish, garnished with Parmesan and green onion curls.

NOTE: To make curls, slice green onion thinly on the bias. Soak in ice water; slices will curl.

» **Spice Blend:**
   3 tablespoons Kosher salt
   1 tablespoon white pepper
   1 tablespoon garlic powder
   5 teaspoons cayenne pepper
   3 teaspoons black pepper
   3 teaspoons ground cumin
   1 1/2 teaspoons dried basil

Combine all ingredients and store in an airtight container.

The Main Event « 125

February 4, 2009

At the old Crouching Lion, the dish they called Slavonic Steak was finished tableside in sauté pans filled with butter and garlic. No wonder it made such an impression.

Robert Denis, now chef at Don Ho's Island Grill, is a longtime employee of the restaurants owned by Fred Livingston. These included the Crouching Lion and the more recent but also closed Tower Grill.

Denis is bringing the steak back for Valentine's Day at Don Ho's. He plans to do all the cooking in the kitchen, though. No tableside sauté.

He gave me his analysis of its appeal: "It's like an M&M: it just melts in the mouth." Plus, "any time you use butter you can't fail."

The deck is rather stacked in favor of this steak: It's filet mignon, heavily dosed in pepper and fresh herbs, marinated overnight in olive oil, pan-seared to seal in the flavor, then coated in butter and garlic. (If you can't afford filet mignon, by the way, you can use New York strip.)

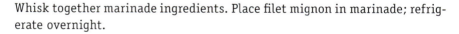

Crouching Lion Slavonic Steak
Serves 4

2 8-ounce pieces filet mignon
2 tablespoons butter
$1/2$ teaspoon minced garlic
Chopped parsley, for garnish

» **Marinade:**
1 cup olive oil
1 tablespoon minced garlic
$1/8$ cup chopped fresh herbs (thyme, rosemary and parsley)
1 tablespoon cracked black pepper

Whisk together marinade ingredients. Place filet mignon in marinade; refrigerate overnight.

The next day, heat sauté pan with a hint of olive oil. Remove steak from marinade and pan-sear until rare.

Gently heat a separate sauté pan. Add butter and garlic, cooking until garlic is lightly brown.

Slice steak and place in pan with butter. Cook to desired doneness. Sprinkle with parsley.

March 12, 2000

When you love Thai food, those flavors stay with you. The heat of the curry, the tang of the kaffir lime, the smooth richness of the coconut milk—it's all the stuff tasty memories are made of.

Carole Thirakoun, chef and co-owner of Thai Valley Cuisine in Kalama Valley, on the Hawai'i Kai end of the island, provided this recipe for a curry that brings all those flavors to the fore.

Thirakoun arrived in Hawai'i in 1980 from Laos, by way of San Francisco. She began her training at age nine in the family kitchen, Laotian cooking being very similar to Thai. Her restaurant résumé includes seven years with Keo Sananikone, as well as time with the Shanghai and Mekong restaurants.

In 1994, she and partner Ron Ching opened Thai Valley Cuisine.

Her focus, Thirakoun says, is on natural tastes, and she uses less oil, more water, in keeping with customers' desires to eat healthier.

Thai Valley Cuisine Green Curry
Serves 2

1 tablespoon prepared green curry paste (May Ploy Brand, if possible)
$1/4$ teaspoon vegetable oil
1 cup water
8 ounces coconut milk
1 cup eggplant, in $3/4$-inch wedges
$1/3$ cup sliced bamboo shoots
$2/3$ cup, long beans, in 1-inch slices
1 2-inch piece lemongrass (use bottom $1/3$ of stalk only)
1 kaffir lime leaf
1 teaspoon sugar
$4 1/2$ tablespoons fish sauce
1 teaspoon lemon juice
10 shrimp, 21/30 count size, peeled
$1/4$ cup Thai sweet basil
$1/4$ large red bell pepper, sliced
Thai red chili pepper, sliced (optional; amount to taste)

Mix green curry paste and oil; cook over medium heat 1 to 2 minutes, stirring to prevent burning. Add water and coconut milk and bring to a boil. Add eggplant, bamboo shoots, beans, lemongrass, lime leaf, sugar, fish sauce and lemon juice. Cook another 3 to 4 minutes, stirring occasionally, until eggplant is tender.

Add shrimp, basil, bell pepper and Thai chili (if using). Reduce heat to medium-low and cook 1 minute, or until shrimp is cooked but still tender.

February 24, 2010

Twice-Cooked Chicken was a menu specialty at A Little Bit of Saigon, a popular Vietnamese restaurant on Maunakea Street in Chinatown in the 1990s. After the restaurant closed owners Duc Nguyen and Minh Na Vu turned their attention to Duc's Bistro. Alas, Twice-Cooked Chicken is not on that menu.

But Vu remembers the recipe, which she developed based on a dish called Coconut Chicken that is popular in Vietnam but not so common in Hawai'i. "When I was in Vietnam we used to go to restaurants to eat and my mother ordered that dish," Vu said. "I fell in love with that dish. I learned how to make it just cooking at home."

The chicken is marinated in a mixture that includes the juice from a fresh young coconut, a step that might be enough to stop an inexperienced home cook right there. But you can get around that task with a trip to a Filipino grocery for a can of coconut water. You want plain coconut water, not the type that's been flavored or sweetened. I found a 10-ounce can for about 60¢ at Pacific Supermarket in Waipahu.

After marinating, the chicken pieces are fried—that's the first-cooked part—then simmered in the marinade, which cooks down to a sauce that coats the chicken—the twice-cooked part. The result is a slightly sweet dish flavored with garlic, shallots and soy sauce. It does not taste of coconut. Coconut water, if you've never taken a sip, has none of the heavy coconut taste of coconut milk.

At the restaurant, the chicken was served on bed of watercress, sliced cucumber, tomatoes and sweet onion.

A Little Bit of Saigon Twice-Cooked Chicken
Serves 4

1 fresh chicken, about 3 pounds, preferably free-range or organic
Vegetable oil for frying

» Marinade:
1 head garlic
$^1/_2$ cup of shallots (about 8 pieces)
2 tablespoons sugar
2 tablespoons fish sauce
2 tablespoons soy sauce
1 teaspoon salt
1 teaspoon pepper
Juice from 1 fresh young coconut, or 1 10-ounce can plain coconut
    water

Wash chicken in salted water, pat dry. Cut into 8 large pieces (leave bones in).

TO MAKE MARINADE: Coarsely chop garlic and shallots. Combine with remaining ingredients except coconut juice. Mix chicken pieces with marinade; add enough coconut juice so chicken is covered. Refrigerate a maximum of 3 hours.

Remove chicken, reserving marinade. Set chicken on paper towels and let air-dry 15 minutes.

Heat oil in sauté pan over medium heat. Fry chicken until golden, lowering heat to prevent burning.

Remove chicken; discard oil. Return chicken to pan with reserved marinade. Cook slowly, turning chicken occasionally until done. Sauce should thicken and coat chicken.

Cut chicken into smaller pieces. Serve topped with remaining sauce in pan.

The Main Event   129

Grand Finale

Never underestimate dessert. The great ones are colorful, luscious and carry the element of surprise.

Sure, everyone's on a diet. But everyone can be tempted, especially if you lie and say your dessert is no-cal. Not that I'm saying you should do that.

Instead, make your dessert so irresistible everyone has to have at least a taste. You've got butter and sugar in your favor, plus possibly chocolate.

It won't be hard.

October 19, 2005

Vicky Cayetano, the former first lady, enjoys baking, but doesn't have a lot for time for it. "In fact, I've never seen my wife bake anything," formerGovernor Ben says.

Mrs. Cayetano, though, says the art runs in her family, her father being big on baking and her mother having a sweet tooth. The result: cakes every week, birthdays or not.

This brings us to her family recipe for an apple cake, which Mrs. Cayetano prepared on an episode of *Hawai'i's Kitchen* in 1998, when she was still first lady.

The cake is more appley than cakey—Mrs. Cayetano says her father was committed to healthy cooking. It's also fairly flat, like a bar cookie, but soft like a cake. There's plenty of apple flavor, spiced with cinnamon and nutmeg. "It's not real attractive," she says, "but it tastes good."

Still, she doesn't expect to be baking one anytime soon. "My husband is the cook now. His stuff is not healthy, to be honest."

Fresh Apple Spice Cake

- 4 cups diced apples
- 1$^1/_3$ cup sugar
- 2 cups sifted flour
- 2 teaspoons cinnamon
- $^1/_2$ teaspoon nutmeg
- $^1/_2$ teaspoon salt
- 2 teaspoons baking soda
- $^2/_3$ cup chopped walnuts
- $^2/_3$ cup golden raisins
- 2 eggs
- $^1/_2$ cup canola oil
- 2 teaspoons vanilla extract

Preheat oven to 350 degrees. Butter a 9-by-13-inch baking pan.

Combine apples, sugar, flour, cinnamon, nutmeg, salt, baking soda, walnuts and raisins. Toss to mix well. Set aside.

Combine eggs, oil and vanilla. Blend until smooth. Add to apple mixture and stir until well-blended. Spread evenly in baking pan. Bake 45 to 60 minutes, until a pick inserted in center comes out clean. Cool.

Serve with whipped cream or ice cream.

September 24, 2008

Want to up the congeniality level at your next staff meeting? Bring a cheesecake. Want to stimulate discussion? Spike the cheesecake with booze.

Worked at our meeting last week. And the point was legitimate: We were trying out a recipe for a B-52 Cheesecake.

The B-52 cocktail, root of this particular evil, is made by layering three liqueurs in a shot glass: at the bottom, a dark and syrupy coffee liqueur such as Kahlua; in the center, Bailey's Irish Cream; on top, a clear orange-flavored liqueur such as Grand Marnier or Cointreau. To keep the layers neat, pour the second and third liqueurs into the glass over the back of a teaspoon.

Converting this essence into a cheesecake simply involves mixing a bit of each liqueur into a part of the batter. You don't end up with clear layers, but you do get some nice flavor.

This recipe is based on a simple cheesecake—I started with one that Kraft Foods developed to better sell cream cheese. No point in getting complicated when the liquor's really the point.

A couple of ingredient notes: You could make your own crust out of chocolate wafer cookies, but a pre-made Oreo pie crust, sold in most grocery stores near the baking goods, makes things simpler. As for the liqueurs, unless you plan to make a lot of cocktails, buy the little airline-size bottles. The three will make one cheesecake and one cocktail.

B-52 Cheesecake

1 Oreo pie crust
3 8-ounce packages cream cheese, softened
1 cup sugar
1 cup sour cream
2 teaspoons vanilla
3 eggs
2 tablespoons orange-flavored liqueur (such as Grand Marnier)
2 tablespoons coffee-flavored liqueur (such as Kahlua)
2 tablespoons Bailey's Irish Cream

Preheat oven to 350 degrees if using a silver 8- or 9-inch springform pan; 325 degrees if using a dark springform pan. Line pan bottom with parchment or waxed paper. Break up pie crust and press into bottom of pan.

Beat cream cheese and sugar on medium speed until well-blended. Add sour cream and vanilla; mix well. Add eggs, one at a time, beating on low speed until blended. Divide batter into 3 parts. Add 1 liqueur to each part. Spread each part over crust, in layers. Bake 60 to 70 minutes, until center is almost set.

Turn oven off and open oven door slightly. Leave cheesecake in oven 1 hour.

Remove; cool completely. Refrigerate at least 4 hours or overnight. Loosen cheesecake from rim of pan; remove rim.

July 26, 2000

A restaurant could be gone, but its best desserts are never forgotten. Such is the case with the Banana Mac-Nut Praline Tart from the Kahala Moon.

Chef/owner Kelvin Ro closed the Kahala Moon in 1998 when his five-year lease ran out. He's landed happily at Kapi'olani Community College, where he is developing curriculum for culinary classes and is involved in special events planning and catering—"real-world-type skills" for the students.

What he doesn't get to do much nowadays is cook, so he was glad to dig out this recipe for his Banana Mac-Nut Praline Tart and put together a sample.

"It was so popular that we did it for Taste of Honolulu," Ro recalls. "Big mistake. Three thousand portions, we had to make. So we ended up doing it like a cobbler and we scooped it out."

In its true form, the tart is like a banana pie with a caramelized filling and a streusel-type topping.

Use ripe bananas, Ro says, the type with brown spots on the skin. "Half-ripe bananas don't do it for me," he says.

Also critical: "Pre-cook" the bananas by marinating them in a pineapple mixture before baking. "You want the banana to start absorbing the acid so it breaks down and it'll be one smooth consistency through the whole thing. The sauce won't penetrate through the whole banana unless you marinate it first."

The three-part recipe may look complicated, but Ro's step-by-step instructions break it down into common-sense pieces. As a bonus, run through it and you'll learn some professional tricks, such as letting the dough sit several hours so the gluten relaxes and the crust is tender—then, after rolling it out, putting the crust in the freezer briefly to firm it up.

Kahala Moon
Banana Mac-Nut Praline Tart

» Orange Crust
   2 cups sifted flour
   1 teaspoon salt
   ¹/₃ cup chilled, unsalted butter
   ¹/₃ cup vegetable shortening
   1 teaspoon orange zest
   2 tablespoons powdered sugar
   5 tablespoons ice water

» **Banana Filling:**
  5 cups ripened bananas
  1/2 cup canned crushed pineapple
  1/4 cup pineapple juice
  1/4 cup butter
  1/2 cup brown sugar
  3 tablespoons fresh-squeezed orange juice
  1 teaspoon cinnamon
  1/2 teaspoon nutmeg
  1 teaspoon vanilla extract
  1/4 teaspoon salt
  2 tablespoons flour

» **Topping:**
  1/2 cup chilled butter
  1/2 cup flour
  1 cup coarsely ground uncooked oatmeal (use food processor or blender)
  1/2 teaspoon salt
  1/2 cup brown sugar
  1/4 cup chopped macadamia nuts
  2 tablespoons white sugar

TO MAKE CRUST: Sift flour a second time, with salt. Add remaining ingredients, except water, and mix until pea-sized granules form. Sprinkle water over dough and mix until dough forms a ball (may not need all 5 tablespoons). Refrigerate at least 12 hours to let gluten relax for a delicate pastry crust.

Roll out dough and place in a 10-inch spring-form tart pan or 2 8-inch pie pans. Place in freezer for 20 minutes to allow dough to cool and firm up again.

TO MAKE FILLING: Combine bananas, pineapple and pineapple juice; let sit 10 minutes.

In a saucepan, melt butter, then mix in brown sugar and orange juice until sugar dissolves. Do not boil or sugar will crystallize. Combine with bananas and remaining ingredients, adding flour last. Pour into chilled crust.

TO MAKE TOPPING: Melt butter and add remaining ingredients, except white sugar. Mix thoroughly and chill at least 2 hours.

Sprinkle over tart, then sprinkle white sugar over all. Bake at 350 degrees, 40-50 minutes until crust is baked and filling is set. Serve with vanilla ice cream and blueberries.

January 2, 2008

Nothing like starting the new year with a food you've never tasted—or, for that matter, never even heard of. In my case that would be Chess Pie.

This regional favorite is a Southern specialty, a cross between a custard pie and a pecan pie without the pecans. Actually, it can have pecans, or other types of nuts, or coconut, lemon, or chocolate. It's one of those traditional dishes that has vamped through time to incorporate lots of variations.

The basic recipe calls for eggs, milk, sugar and butter—like a custard pie—with cornmeal for thickening and vinegar for some acidic twang that somewhat moderates the sweetness. Sometimes the vinegar and milk are replaced by buttermilk; sometimes the cornmeal by flour.

I opted to try one with some brown sugar, which yielded a really nice toffee flavor, but if you prefer a lighter taste, go with all white sugar. It's basically a pantry pie—the ingredients are likely to be in your fridge and cupboard and are easily mixed together. What emerged from my oven was one of the prettiest things I've ever baked, all puffy and golden.

In time the puffiness settled and the pie just looked like a pie. A nice pie, though. Sweet, rich and creamy, with the cornmeal giving it a unique texture.

As for that name.... Here I crib from Diana Rattray, a Mississippi cook who writes about Southern cooking for About.com. She says the name "chess" could be an allusion to cheese; there's no cheese in the pie but it is sort of cheesecake-like in texture. Or it could have been named after the pie chest in which it was stored.

Her best explanation, though, is this: Husband asks wife what kind of pie it is and she says, "I don't know. It's ches' pie."

Chess Pie

1/2 cup butter, softened
1 cup sugar
1/2 cup brown sugar
4 eggs, beaten
1 tablespoon cornmeal
1/4 cup evaporated milk
2 teaspoons vanilla extract
1 tablespoon white vinegar
1 unbaked 9-inch pie shell

Preheat oven to 350 degrees

Cream butter and sugars. Mix in eggs, then add remaining ingredients and stir until smooth. Pour into pie shell. Bake 30 minutes, until center is set and top is golden.

April 1, 2009

This adventure began with a request for a recipe for Hawaiian coconut candy—the red, sugar-covered balls that you can buy in crack-seed stores.

I found a recipe in a cookbook published in 1983 by the Kamehameha Schools, *Oldies But Goodies*, credited to Tamar Luke Panee, class of 1953. All you do is mix coconut flakes with corn syrup, roll it into balls, and then cover the balls in colored sugar.

Very simple—and close—but not quite right.

So I went to a crack-seed store and picked up a small bag of the real stuff, and there was the clue in the ingredient list: unsweetened desiccated coconut. The usual baker's coconut found in supermarkets is sweetened and shredded, with the pieces fairly large. To find unsweetened dried coconut, sometimes called macaroon coconut, try a health-food store, where it's often sold among the bulk goods. I got some at Down to Earth.

These smaller, drier flakes produce a candy very much like the commercial version, although it needs to be refrigerated. Like many homemade candies, it's not an exact match for the original, but in some ways it's better—softer and not as sugary.

Coconut Candy
Makes about 48 balls

2 cups unsweetened macaroon coconut (see note)
$^1/_2$ cup light corn syrup
$^1/_4$ cup sugar
Red food coloring

Combine coconut with corn syrup and mix thoroughly, adding a little more syrup if needed to evenly coat the flakes. Roll into $^1/_2$-inch balls, squeezing the mixture to compress.

Color sugar by adding 1 or 2 drops of coloring and mixing well.

Roll balls in sugar. Chill at least 1 hour.

NOTE: Find unsweetened dried coconut in health-food stores, generally sold in bulk. If you have a choice, buy the finest flakes available.

January 20, 2010

Saturday, January 23, is National Pie Day, so declared by the National Pie Council as a way of "helping people across the nation recall the simple pleasure of presenting a pie as a gesture of kindness."

Perhaps you have never heard of the day, the council or the inherent kindliness of pie, but think about it: When someone shares a pie, or better yet, takes one warm from the oven, your mind says, "Yah, pie!" or, "Yum, pie!" or otherwise undergoes a positive brain synapse.

So here's my suggestion: Have a pie buffet—at the office, a family gathering or any other place where humans and their appetites are expected. Do it for the fun of it or to celebrate someone's special day.

We had one yesterday in the newsroom and assembled a collection of twenty-seven pies, from pumpkin to pecan to peach to pizza (yes, pizza pies count).

My contribution was a coconut cream, a lovely pie, if I do say so myself, although all the credit goes to Janet Ness, who sent the recipe.

"My mother made this pie from a recipe in the *Ono Kau Kau* cookbook published by Central Union Church so many years ago that my copy is in tatters," Ness wrote. "This was my husband's favorite pie, and he had to have it for his birthday. Now my daughter also requires it and although she lives in Missouri now, manages to find fresh coconut."

Ness notes that the recipe is not quick and easy; you've got to make custard, whip cream, beat up a meringue. You should also start with a fresh coconut, although I cheated and used frozen grated coconut, available in Filipino markets. Don't use sweetened baker's coconut from the supermarket.

Happy Pie Day to you.

Coconut Cream Pie

1 envelope unflavored gelatin
1²/₃ cup milk, divided use
¹/₄ cup flour
¹/₂ cup sugar, divided use
1/8 teaspoon salt
3 egg yolks
1 cup whipping cream
1¹/₂ cups fresh grated coconut
Baked 10-inch pie shell

» Meringue:
3 egg whites
6 tablespoons sugar

Dissolve gelatin in ¹/₄ cup milk. Set aside.

Combine rest of milk slowly with flour, ¹/₄ cup sugar and salt. Cook in top of double boiler over simmering water, stirring until smooth and thick, 10 to 15 minutes.

Beat egg yolks with remaining ¹/₄ cup sugar. Add slowly to mixture in double boiler, whisking steadily, and cook 3 more minutes, making a custard.

Remove from heat and whisk in gelatin (remove any gelatin clumps). Let cool, whisking occasionally to keep smooth.

TO MAKE MERINGUE: Beat egg whites, adding sugar gradually, until stiff peaks form. Fold into cooled custard.

Whip cream until light and fluffy. Fold half of the whipped cream and most of the coconut into custard (reserve some for garnish). Pour into pie shell and refrigerate until firm.

Before serving, cover pie with rest of whipped cream (sweetened with powdered sugar if desired) and sprinkle with extra coconut.

Grand Finale « 139

September 30, 2009

Some things you have to take on faith. For example, I've come to accept that custard pies baked in Hawai'i taste different from those elsewhere. This is based not on empirical evidence, but on the many, many inquiries I've received from former Hawai'i people missing "the good kine" custard pie.

One of my readers, who's been living in Florida for twelve years, says she thinks she can quantify the difference: "You just can't find a custard pie around here that has a creamy filling and flaky crust. Most times, the pies taste like cooked eggs, rather than sweet, creamy, with just a hint of vanilla!"

To the rescue: Henry Shun, a retired professional baker, who collected many of his local-style recipes into a booklet, *Seasons of Baking*, in 2001.

Shun says most standard custard pie recipes call for fresh milk, whereas the traditional local recipe uses evaporated milk, which provides more richness. The formula, he says, is 1 part evaporated milk to 1 part water. Don't try to bulk up the taste by substituting fresh milk for the water; he says the flavor will be wrong.

Beyond that the fine-tuning is in the technique. Shun's filling is made a day ahead, which makes it nice and glossy. Bubbles will rise to the surface, where you skim them off—this way your baked pie won't have air pockets or a pocked surface. Also, Shun suggests filling the pie shell a bit short of the rim. Bake 10 minutes, then add more filling. This keeps the center from sinking.

Also included here is Shun's crust recipe. There are simpler recipes, but this is a professional's recipe, designed for better results by taking more care.

One tip: if your crust puffs up in the bottom, poke a few small holes in the bottom of your pie pan with an ice pick (the pan can still be reused). The holes let hot air escape rather than push up into your crust. Obviously you can't do this with a glass pan.

My pie baked up beautifully, looking just like it came from a bakery. And it did indeed taste rich, creamy, and not at all eggy.

Island-Style Custard Pie

» **Filling:**
5 large eggs
$3/4$ cup sugar
$2^1/_2$ tablespoons cornstarch
$1^1/_2$ cups evaporated milk
$1^1/_2$ cups water
2 teaspoons vanilla
$1/_8$ teaspoon salt

» Crust:

2¹/₈ cups pastry flour (see note)
³/₄ cup plus 1 tablespoon shortening or butter
¹/₄ cup plus 2 tablespoons water
¹/₂ teaspoon salt
1 tablespoon sugar

TO MAKE FILLING: Break eggs into mixing bowl. Combine sugar with corn-starch. Whisk into eggs until incorporated. Continue to whisk for 1 minute. Add evaporated milk, water, vanilla and salt. Mix until well-incorporated. Cover bowl and refrigerate overnight.

TO MAKE CRUST: Place 2 cups flour in bowl with shortening or butter. Cut shortening into flour (using pastry cutter or two butter knives) until mix-ture forms pea-size lumps.

Combine water, salt and sugar with remaining flour to make soft paste. Add to flour/shortening mixture and combine to form ball. Roll into a log about 3 inches in diameter, cover with waxed paper and chill overnight.

The next day, work dough slightly to blend in any lumps of shortening. Don't worry about overmixing. No lumps should remain, or they will melt and cre-ate raw spots in the crust.

Divide dough into a ball. Roll out dough to fit your pie pan. Place in pan, tap-ping so dough is flush with pan. Trim edges with plastic knife and crimp.

Preheat oven to 400 degrees.

Skim off any bubbles from top of filling. Stir gently to blend in cornstarch settled on bottom of bowl. Do not create bubbles while stirring. Pour filling into pie shell, filling it ¹/₄ inch from rim. Bake 10 minutes, then add more filling, up to the rim of the pie shell.

Continue baking about 20 minutes longer, until done. Check frequently: Nudge the pie gently; if it ripples near the center, it is not quite ready. Do not overbake. If the pie puffs up in the center, you've baked it too long, and your filling will be full of holes and watery (what a shame).

NOTE: Pastry flour is a low-protein flour that might be hard to find. Sub-stitute with a mixture of 3³/₄ cups all-purpose flour combined with ¹/₂ cup cornstarch.

Grand Finale   141

April 29, 2009

As a longtime volunteer for various school groups (three kids—that's a LOT of school carnivals), I know well the value of a parent with specialized skills who is willing to donate them to the cause.

So I salute the anonymous cafeteria manager who gives his cookie-baking talent to Roosevelt High School's Project Graduation.

Leila Tamashiro, treasurer for Friends of Roosevelt Project Grad, said the baker would prefer that his name not be known but was happy to share his recipe for Frosted Flake Chocolate Chip Cookies, which have been all the rage at several of the group's fundraisers.

Now, this is a great cookie. Or was. My four test batches disappeared from the newsroom food table in minutes. Literally.

About the recipe: it has no eggs or liquid (this is NOT a mistake). This seems to keep the flakes crunchy. Also, the baking temperature is low, 325 degrees, which seems to make the cookie very crunchy, but mine didn't brown much, even after 30 minutes. (By the way, DON'T bake yours for 30 minutes. When they cool they'll be rock hard. Try 20 minutes—the cookies will still be soft, but they'll firm up as they cool.)

Frosted Flake Chocolate Chip Cookies

Makes about 2 dozen

4 cups Frosted Flakes
2 sticks (1 cup) butter
$^3/_4$ cup sugar
1 teaspoon vanilla
2 cups flour
1 teaspoon baking soda
$^1/_2$ cup chocolate chips

Preheat oven to 325 degrees. Line a cookie sheet with parchment.

Crush frosted flakes lightly (until they compress to about 3 cups; don't make them too fine).

Cream butter and sugar until fluffy. Add vanilla.

Combine flour and baking soda; gradually add to butter mixture and stir to combine. Fold in crushed frosted flakes and chocolate chips. Mixture will be crumbly. It's best to use your hands to make sure ingredients combine evenly. Roll 2-tablespoon portions of dough into balls and place on cookie sheet. Flatten slightly.

Bake about 20 minutes, until lightly brown. Cookies will be soft but will firm up as they cool. Don't overbake or cookies will become very hard.

April 20, 2005

Last week I received a no-strings-attached special offer via e-mail. And it wasn't spam. Ryan Abregano offered to solve a recipe mystery for me, based on his own research and experimentation.

Never one to pass up a good deal, I pulled out a fresh request from a reader who wanted to make green tea mousse. Not ice cream; a light, cool mousse.

I passed the challenge on to Abregano and figured I might never hear from him again. But two days later, there it was: his recipe for mousse.

Abregano attended the Culinary Institute of America in New York, but had to put his cooking career on hold five years ago to come back to Hawai'i and help his family. But he says he studies and writes down cooking ideas while working at a car dealership, then goes home and tries them out.

This mousse formula began with Abregano's research into basic mousse and green tea ice cream recipes.

Feel free to vamp on his basic recipe. He says he aimed for a very strong tea flavor, but if you want something subtler, try using fewer leaves or a shorter steeping time.

Green Tea Mousse

¹/₂ cup loose green tea
2 cups hot water
6 egg yolks
2 tablespoons sugar
1¹/₂ cups heavy cream

» Meringue:
6 egg whites
1¹/₄ cups sugar

Steep tea in hot water until dark, 5 to 10 minutes. Strain.

In a non-reactive metal bowl, combine yolks and sugar. Place bowl over a pan of simmering water, making sure the bowl is not touching water. Whisk continuously until mixture reaches 166 degrees on a candy thermometer.

Remove from heat. Beat with an electric mixer 5 minutes, until cool and thick. Add ¹/₄ cup of the green tea and beat until combined.

In a separate bowl, beat cream until stiff peaks form. Fold into yolk mixture. Cover and chill in freezer overnight. Mixture will firm up, but will not harden like ice cream.

The next day, make meringue: Beat egg whites with sugar until stiff peaks form. Remove mousse from freezer and whip in meringue.

November 4, 2009

A coconut macaroon is almost pure shredded coconut, held together by sheer force of will—OK, and maybe some egg whites.

This cookie is basically a meringue, ideally a light cloud of sweetness that's crisp on the outside and chewy on the inside.

This recipe takes the approach of toasting the coconut, which mellows the flavor and helps provide outer crunch. This makes them a toasty brown all over, not the virgin white you might be used to.

Toasted Coconut Macaroons
Makes 2 dozen

4 egg whites
Pinch salt
1½ cups powdered sugar
1 teaspoon vanilla or almond extract
4 cups shredded sweetened coconut, toasted (see note)

Preheat oven to 325 degrees. Line 2 cookies sheets with baker's parchment.

Whisk egg whites and salt until foamy. Gradually add sugar, whisking rapidly until mixture is smooth and thick (use a mixer if you like, but I've found it's just as fast to whip it by hand and saves on dishes).

Fold in vanilla, then coconut. Stir well to moisten all the coconut.

Using wet hands, form the mixture into tablespoon-size mounds and place on cookie sheets, an inch or so apart. Bake 15 to 20 minutes. Cookies should be firm but still yield to the touch. Slip parchment onto rack to cool, then peel cookies off paper.

NOTE: Toast coconut in dry skillet over medium heat, stirring until golden.

October 24, 2007

The full moon approaches, as does Halloween, which may make you want to howl at the sky, but don't do that. Instead, express some autumnal enthusiasm through the moon cake.

This Chinese treat is traditional at the time of the Harvest Moon—actually that was last month, which makes me thirty days late. But it so happens that the full moon tomorrow will be the biggest full moon of the year, making this quite a fortuitous—as well as tasty—recipe.

The pastry for this recipe is adapted from one by Nina Simonds, the author of several books on Chinese cooking.

It turns out it's not that hard to make your own moon cakes, once you find all the right stuff: a moon cake mold and some pre-made bean paste. Both of these, and the salted duck eggs that often are tucked into the cakes, can be found at Bo Wah Trading Co. on Maunakea Street, between Hotel and King.

A wooden mold goes for $15. One-pound bags of bean paste and six-packs of precooked duck eggs are about $2 each. It can be hard to search the crowded shelves, but ask and you'll be pointed in the right direction.

Moon Cakes
Makes 20 cakes

» **Crust:**
3/4 cup unsalted butter
4 cups flour
3/4 cup powdered milk
1 teaspoon salt
1 tablespoon baking powder
3 large eggs
1¼ cups sugar
1½ teaspoons vanilla extract

» **Filling 1:**
2 cups sweetened bean paste
Yolks from 20 salted duck eggs, optional

» **Filling 2:**
1 cup apricot preserves (about 12 ounces)
1¼ cup chopped dates
1 cup raisins

» **Glaze:**
1 large egg, lightly beaten with 2 tablespoons water

146   » Grand Finale

TO MAKE CRUST: Melt butter, then let cool to room temperature.

Combine flour, powdered milk, salt and baking powder.

Beat eggs and sugar vigorously 5 minutes. Beat in butter and vanilla, then gradually fold in dry ingredients to form a rough dough. Turn onto a lightly floured surface and knead until a smooth dough forms. Roll into 2 logs and cut into 20 pieces (10 pieces per log).

Preheat oven to 375 degrees. Lightly grease 2 baking sheets. Dust moon cake mold with flour. Use fingers to press each piece of dough into a thin, 4-inch circle. Press the edges even thinner.

FOR FILLING 1: Wrap a yolk inside a 2-tablespoon scoop of bean paste and place in center of dough circle. Gather up edges of dough to enclose filling and pinch to seal. Roll cake into a ball. Press ball into mold. Tap mold on sides to release cake. Arrange cakes 1 inch apart on baking sheets.

FOR FILLING 2: Combine ingredients; divide into 20 portions. Place a portion into center of circles of dough and form cakes as with Filling 1.

Brush cakes generously with glaze on tops and sides. Bake 20 to 30 minutes, until golden brown.

Grand Finale

September 9, 2009

You can spend a lifetime learning the rules of baking, then someone presents you with something delicious, along with a recipe that ignores the rules.

In this case the rule is "Always preheat." This is supposed to ensure that the oven is at the right temperature, ready to turn your batter into cake, or your dough into cookies.

But while researching a request for a guaranteed moist pound cake I found this recipe in a cookbook called *America's Best Lost Recipes* (2007, America's Test Kitchen), by the editors of *Cook's Country* magazine, a group that tests, tests, and retests recipes.

The key to a moist cake with a slightly crunchy crust was to start with a cold oven, the editors insisted.

The recipe that follows is based closely on that original. I've made it a few times and it is exceptional.

I had a happy accident with my first cake: when unmolding it, a big chunk broke off. I stuck it back on, and such is the magical moistness of this cake that it has adhesive qualities: The pieces fused together overnight, enough that the cake was presentable and could be sliced and served without falling apart.

This cake has a lovely, light taste that deepens and improves after a day or so. A spoonful of whipped cream, ice cream, or fruit, or a sprinkle of powdered sugar would be a nice touch, but the cake is addictive as is.

Cold Oven Pound Cake

3 cups flour
$1/2$ teaspoon salt
1 cup skim milk
1 teaspoon vanilla extract
5 large eggs, separated, at room temperature
2 sticks butter, softened
$1/2$ cup vegetable shortening
3 cups sugar

Grease and flour a 12-cup tube or bundt pan.

Whisk together flour and salt. Whisk milk, vanilla and egg yolks in another bowl.

Beat egg whites to soft peaks.

Beat butter, shortening and sugar together until fluffy. Reduce speed to low and gradually add flour and milk mixture, beating after each addition until combined. Fold in egg whites.

Scrape batter into prepared pan and place in cold oven, on rack in middle position. Turn oven on to 300 degrees and bake 45 minutes.

Increase heat to 325 and bake another 45 minutes, until cake tests done. Cool cake in pan 20 minutes (if you let the cake sit longer the crust won't have as much crunch). Run a knife around edges to loosen, then turn cake onto a rack to cool completely.

Grand Finale « 149

September 23, 2009

More birthdays is the theme here. More birthdays and beets.

The American Cancer Society and the Culinary Institute of America teamed up to come up with a celebration-worthy cake lower in fat and calories through a contest among CIA students. Healthier eating means less cancer and more birthdays for more people—get it?

The winner, judged by a panel that included Duff Goldman of the *Ace of Cakes* television show, was Alexandra Mudry, for a slimmed down Red Velvet Cake made with roasted beets.

The Hawai'i chapter of the cancer society served Murdry's cake in cupcake form at its fiftieth birthday celebration. It was a light, moist, tasty cake, but not much like a traditional red velvet—for one thing, it was pink, not red. If you do take on this rather ambitious recipe, do it for the sake of its high flavor and low fat, not because you crave red velvet.

New Red Velvet Cake

$^1/_2$ **cup canola oil**
2 large eggs
2 large egg whites
1 cup sugar
1 teaspoon instant espresso powder or instant coffee
3 ounces unsweetened chocolate, melted
$^1/_2$ **cup unsweetened cocoa powder**
$^1/_2$ **cup unsweetened applesauce**
1 cup dried cherries
$^3/_4$ **cup all-purpose flour**
$^3/_4$ **cup whole-wheat flour**
$^1/_4$ **cup quinoa flour (see note)**
1$^1/_2$ teaspoons baking soda
$^1/_2$ **teaspoon salt**

» Beet Purée
3 large or 5 small beets (see note)
1 tablespoon canola oil
1 to 2 tablespoons water

» Cream Cheese Frosting:
24 ounces reduced-fat cream cheese, at room temperature
2 teaspoons vanilla extract
1$^1/_2$ cups powdered sugar

Preheat oven to 375 degrees. Trim beets and place on foil- or parchment-lined baking pan. Drizzle with canola oil. Roast until tender, about 2 hours. Cool, then peel and purée in blender or food processor with water until smooth. You should have 2 cups. Set aside (may be made ahead and refrigerated).

Preheat oven to 375 degrees. Line cupcake pans with paper liners (or use 2 8-inch round cake pans or a 9-by-13-inch pan greased and floured).

Beat oil, eggs, egg white and sugar on medium speed until smooth and light colored.

Combine espresso powder with melted chocolate. Lower mixer speed and drizzle chocolate into egg mixture.

In a separate bowl combine cocoa powder, applesauce and beet purée. Add to egg mixture on medium speed. Fold in cherries. Mix again.

Sift together flours, baking soda and salt. Gently fold into previous mixture. Do not overmix or cake will be tough. Pour into baking cups and bake 20 to 25 minutes (40 to 45 minutes for cakes). Cool, then frost.

TO MAKE FROSTING: Beat cream cheese and vanilla until smooth, 1 to 2 minutes.

Add powdered sguar and cream utnil smooth. Do not overmix or frosting will be too soft to spread.

NOTES: Quinoa flour may be found in natural-foods stores, or substitute 1 cup all-purpose flour combined with ¾ cup whole-wheat flour. Canned beets may be used in place of fresh, but be sure they are not seasoned.

August 21, 2002

Rum has overtaken Harry Matsuno's life. This would be a bad thing if he were drinking it, but he's pouring it into bundt cakes that he gives away, thereby spreading the joy of rum to the world.

"You are the recipient of Rum Cake No. 279 for the year 2002," read a card delivered with a cake last week.

Given that last Wednesday was the 226th day of the year, you figure the man is averaging more than a cake a day. And that's just until the holiday season, when Matsuno's baking kicks into overdrive.

Last year at Christmas, Matsuno baked eighty rum cakes. They went two at a time into his oven and while each pair was baking, he was getting two more ready. Some weekends, he'd do twenty-four, right there in his home kitchen, using the same recipe and the same four bundt pans he's used for about twenty years.

Matsuno is well on pace to meet his goal for this year: "I'm shooting for five hundred."

So who is this guy with this obsessive baking hobby?

Matsuno is president of Safeguard Services, which provides security guards for such properties as Bank of Hawai'i and the Pearl Highlands and Waikele shopping centers. The company, formed after Matsuno retired from the Army, is twenty years old and employs six hundred guards.

He started out baking for family and friends at Christmas, using a friend's recipe that he adapted. Then, he thought, "Why just holidays? I hadn't heard anything about restrictions." Rum cakes became a year-round concern, baked for clients as thank-you gifts.

He buys light rum in half-gallon bottles at Costco, and keeps his cupboard stocked with yellow cake mix and instant vanilla pudding—the main building blocks of his recipe.

So, now we understand what Matsuno does and how. But ...

"Why? That's a good question. My wife said, 'Do the cakes do any good for you?' I said, 'They don't do any harm.' She didn't say anything after that."

152 » Grand Finale

Harry's Famous Rum Cake

12 walnut halves, chopped
$\frac{1}{2}$ cup water
$\frac{1}{2}$ cup vegetable oil
$\frac{1}{2}$ cup rum
4 eggs
1 teaspoon vanilla
1 large box instant vanilla instant pudding
1 box yellow cake mix (preferably Duncan Hines)

» **Glaze and glazed nuts:**
1 stick butter
$\frac{3}{4}$ cup of sugar
$\frac{1}{2}$ cup rum
2 cups walnuts or almonds

Preheat oven to 325 degrees. Spray a bundt cake pan with cooking oil spray. Arrange nuts evenly in bottom of pan.

Combine water, oil, rum, eggs and vanilla. Stir in pudding mix, then cake mix. Mix all ingredients and pour into bundt pan. Bake 55 minutes to one hour.

Meanwhile, make glaze: In saucepan, melt butter, then add sugar. Stir while bringing mixture to a boil. Add rum. Continue to boil, depending on how much alcohol you want burned off. All the alcohol will burn off in 2 minutes.

Remove cake from oven. Pour $\frac{1}{2}$ of glaze into the edges of the pan and let it soak in for a few minutes. Invert pan onto plate and remove cake. Spoon $\frac{1}{2}$ of remaining glaze over cake.

Stir the walnuts or almonds into the remaining glaze until well-coated. Spoon glazed nuts into middle of cake.

Grand Finale » 153

June 4, 2003

Shortbread is a traditional Scottish cookie, tied to the Christmas and New Year's holidays. With its high butter quotient, shortbread is a rich, satisfying treat.

From out of Scotland, though, this cookie has been adopted by the world. The locally popular macadamia nut version is clear evidence of how far the basic formula has traveled.

Shortbread is a very simple thing: flour, sugar, butter. No eggs, even. Most basic recipes can accommodate a half-cup or so of any type of nuts. The recipe can be dressed up, though. The recipes that follow reflect both types: a basic version and a fancier one that bakes up light and delicate, thanks to the use of cake flour in the mix.

Macadamia Nut Shortbread

2 cups flour
$^1/_2$ cup sugar
1 cup (2 sticks) butter, chilled, cut in small cubes
$^3/_4$ cup chopped macadamia nuts

Preheat oven to 350 degrees.

Combine flour and sugar. Cut in butter until texture is sandy. Fold in nuts. Press into a 9-by-13-inch pan and bake 15 to 20 minutes.

Cool slightly, then cut into squares.

Melt-in-Your-Mouth Macadamia Shortbread
Makes about 56 cookies

2 cups (4 sticks) butter, softened
1 cup plus 2 tablespoons sugar
1 teaspoon vanilla extract
$^1/_2$ teaspoon salt
3 cups plus 3 tablespoons flour
1 cup cake flour
1$^3/_4$ cups finely chopped macadamia nuts
$^1/_4$ cup raw sugar

Preheat oven to 350 degrees. Lightly oil 2 baking sheets.

Cream butter, sugar, vanilla and salt until light and fluffy. Add flour and cake flour; beat until smooth.

Combine nuts and raw sugar in a small bowl. Form dough into 1-inch balls and roll in nut-sugar mixture. Place 2 inches apart on baking sheets. Bake 15 minutes or until golden brown.

Grand Finale « 155

February 4, 2004

Frances Pons says none of her recipes are secrets—in fact, she adapts most from *Joy of Cooking* or an old Good Housekeeping cookbook. It's just that she makes 'em tiny and spends a lot of time decorating.

And sometimes she'll boost the flavorings—after all, you have to make a complete impression in just one bite.

The key, she says, is patience, especially when it comes to unmolding. She suggests refrigerating the pastries several hours, then carefully unmolding, using a sharp knife to loosen the sides first.

She created this taro cheesecake recipe in response to a reader's request. Pons notes that different brands of taro produce different colors. The Poi Co.'s product turned out a pale beige cheesecake, while Hale'iwa Poi resulted in the more traditional purple, which she intensified with a drop of blue food coloring.

Miniature Taro Cheesecake
Makes about 45 cheesecakes

1 pound cream cheese, at room temperature
1 cup sugar
1 teaspoon vanilla extract
1 cup poi
2 eggs, at room temperature

» **Crust:**
2 cups graham cracker or shortbread cookie crumbs
¼ cup sugar
½ cup melted unsalted butter

Preheat oven to 300 degrees. Lightly grease 4 mini-muffin pans.

TO MAKE CRUST: Combine all ingredients. Press dough into bottoms of cups in muffin pans.

Beat cream cheese, sugar and vanilla on low speed until smooth. Scrape sides of bowl and beaters; beat some more. Add taro and beat until smooth, scraping again. Add eggs one at a time, blending the first in completely before adding the next. Fill muffin cups ¾ full with batter. Bake 35 minutes.

Cool to room temperature, then refrigerate overnight before unmolding.

August 16, 2006

The Chinese Tea Cookie—Kong Sui Ban—has proven an elusive recipe. I have requests on file dating to 2001, and over the years I've printed several pleas for the recipe. No one came through until a few weeks ago, when three readers all turned up with family recipes.

All the recipes were similar, with basic ingredients save one: wong tong, or Chinese brown sugar. I got good results substituting regular brown sugar, but I like wong tong for the flavor and sense of tradition.

These cookies won't win any beauty contests—they're nondescript, tan discs—but the flavor is superior. Don't expect an exact duplicate of what you're used to buying in Chinatown (where they're sometimes sold as "tea cakes"), but the texture's a match and the taste is really, really close.

One baking note: these cookies are typically very large, 3 inches across or even more. You might want to make them smaller—better for munching.

Chinese Tea Cookies
Makes 20 large cookies

1 cup water
5 slabs (about 13 ounces) wong tong (Chinese brown sugar; see note)
$1/2$ cup white sugar
$5^1/2$ cups flour
2 tablespoons baking powder
$1/4$ cup honey
1 cup vegetable oil
2 eggs

Bring water to boil. Break wong tong into pieces and add to water. Stir to dissolve. Remove from heat and stir in white sugar to dissolve.

Whisk together flour and baking powder.

Combine honey and oil; beat in eggs. Add to flour mixture and stir to combine. Add sugar syrup and mix until smooth. Let rest 1 hour.

Preheat oven to 350 degrees. Cover cookie sheets with baking parchment.

Scoop dough onto cookie sheets and press flat (about $1/2$ inch thick). Cookies should be 3 inches wide for traditional size, but it's OK to make them smaller. Bake 12 to 15 minutes.

Cool slightly on cookie sheet, then move cookies to a rack.

NOTE: Wong tong is sold in blocks in most grocery stores in Chinatown. Or, $1^1/2$ cups brown sugar may be used in place of wong tong.

December 24, 2008

It's amazing how many random facts there are in the world, just waiting to jump up and poke you in the eye. Take, for example, the Japanese Christmas Cake.

A week before Christmas, I received a request for a recipe. Never having heard of such a thing, I had no recipe in my back pocket, but after asking around and Googling around, the answer was easy enough to determine. The Japanese Christmas Cake is a sponge cake layered with whipped cream and fruit, typically red berries. Although Japan is not a Christian nation, the trappings of the holiday are important, and this cake has become one of them.

A traditional sponge cake is made with no fat beyond what's in the egg yolks and no chemical leaveners (although this recipe uses baking powder to help guarantee results). The cake relies on trapped air and steam to make it light.

Technique is important, so pay attention to detail (I didn't the first time, and my cake did not rise to its full potential). This is the type of cake that will improve as you, the baker, try and try again. Key elements:

- Don't grease the pan. The batter will rise better when the sides of the pan are dry.

- Beat the egg yolks until light and foamy, then add sugar gradually and continue to beat until thick. *Joy of Cooking* suggests beating until a spoonful of the mixture dropped back into the bowl will stay suspended for a moment above the rest of the yolk-sugar mix.

- Warm the yolk mixture, either by adding hot water, or by beating over a bowl of hot water. This helps increase volume.

- Fold in the flour gently, the idea being to keep the air in the batter.

158 » Grand Finale

Japanese Christmas Cake

1 cup sifted cake flour
1^1/$_2$ teaspoons baking powder
^{1}/$_4$ teaspoon salt
3 eggs, separated
1 cup sugar
^{1}/$_4$ cup boiling water
1 teaspoon vanilla extract
^{1}/$_4$ teaspoon cream of tartar

» Topping:
2 cups whipping cream
1 tablespoon powdered sugar
Sliced strawberries or other fruit

Preheat oven to 350 degrees. Line the bottoms of two 8- or 9-inch cake pans with parchment paper. Do not grease pans.

Combine flour, baking powder and salt; set aside.

Beat egg yolks on medium-high speed until thickened, about a minute. Gradually beat in sugar. Continue beating 3 minutes, or until thick and pale.

Beat in water, then vanilla. Gently fold in dry ingredients.

In a clean, dry bowl and using clean beaters, beat egg whites and cream of tartar until stiff peaks form. Gently fold whites into batter, in 2 batches. Pour batter into prepared pans and bake 20 minutes, or until a pick inserted into center comes out clean.

TO MAKE TOPPING: Whip cream and sugar on high speed until fluffy. Don't overbeat or mixture will separate. For best results, chill bowl and beaters 10 minutes in freezer before beating.

TO ASSEMBLE CAKE: Spread whipped cream between cake layers and top with fruit. Spread more whipped cream on top of cake and decorate with fruit. Sides may be covered with whipped cream or left bare.

June 11, 2008

I'm going to assume that anyone who sets out to make a tofu pie isn't really interested in a pie that tastes like tofu.

Chances are they're in it for the health benefits. Tofu pies mimic chiffon pies, without the eggs or cream, although nondairy whipped toppings are standard. The usual formula calls for a box of Jell-O, which is whipped in with tofu, and somehow it all magically creates a creamy, chiffon-like filling.

One of my correspondents asked for my best recipe for a tofu pie. Truth is, until last week I'd never made one; I'd only tasted pies made by others, and none were worth a return visit. They all had that soybeany aftertaste that's great in plain tofu, but, sheesh, keep it outta my desserts.

The solution seems to be to pick a flavor that's strong enough to mask the tofu. I suggest lemon or lime, with added citrus juice to pump up the tartness. One of my friends even stirs in a small can of crushed pineapple (drained), to disguise things even more.

I made up a lemon pie, based on a recipe from *The Tastes and Tales of Mōʻiliʻili* (fifth printing, 2005, $14.95), which passed my own taste test (no tofu flavor) and I put it out on the office food table without telling anyone what it was. Of course, everything eventually gets eaten off that table, but this pie was cleaned up with respectable speed, no one suspecting tofu. I'd take that as a positive review.

Lemon Tofu Pie

1 3-ounce box lemon-flavored gelatin
1 cup hot water
2 tablespoons lemon juice
10 ounces soft tofu
1 8-ounce container non-dairy whipped topping (such as Cool Whip)
1 prepared graham-cracker pie crust

Combine gelatin, hot water and lemon juice; stir to dissolve gelatin. Refrigerate 20 to 30 minutes until slightly thickened.

Meanwhile, cut tofu in chunks and place in colander to drain. Push on tofu with palm to squeeze out as much liquid as possible.

Beat tofu, gradually adding whipped topping. Mixture may be grainy; do not be alarmed. Fold in gelatin; stir until smooth. Pour into pie crust and refrigerate until firm, 3 to 4 hours.

Garnish with more whipped topping if desired.

NOTE: Any flavor of gelatin may be used in place of lemon, but keep the lemon juice.

February 3, 1999

What exactly is a yellow cake? I mean, you have your chocolate cakes, which are obvious in their source of flavor and color; and your white cakes, which are basically vanilla flavored. Yellow cakes get that way because of the egg yolks. White cakes don't have any, and basic butter cakes have fewer. This cake calls for as many as 5 yolks.

Normally, when I need a yellow cake my solution is Duncan Hines mix-in-a-box. Especially good if you substitute applesauce for the oil. But then, no one needs my help with that.

Turns out this scratch cake is pretty simple. The recipe is based one that took first prize at the Maui County Fair in the 1950s, so it's a guaranteed winner.

Yellow Cake

- 1 cup shortening
- 2 cups sugar
- 4 eggs (or 2 yolks and 3 whole eggs)
- 3 cups sifted flour
- 3 teaspoons baking powder
- 1/2 teaspoon salt
- 3/4 cup milk
- 1 teaspoon lemon extract
- 1 teaspoon vanilla extract

Preheat oven to 350 degrees. Grease and flour a 9-by-13 inch pan

Cream shortening and sugar; add eggs one at a time and beat well.

Sift flour, baking powder and salt together and add to creamed mixture alternately with milk and flavorings.

Bake 35 to 45 minutes, or until done.

Recipe Index

5 A Day Sushi, 89

A

A Little Bit of Saigon Twice-Cooked Chicken, 129
Aaron's Caper Vinaigrette, 72
Alley Restaurant Coca-Cola Turkey, 109
Anchovy Salad Dressing, 74
Angelo Pietro Chicken and Spinach Spaghetti, 101
Angelo Pietro Raw Potato Salad, 55
Ashitibichi, 121

B

B-52 Cheesecake, 133
Bara Sushi, 88
Barbecued Chicken, 9
Barbecued Lamb Chops, 107
Beef with Pickled Mustard Cabbage, 2
Beer-Battered Maui Onion Rings, 45
Big City Diner Oatmeal Cakes, 26
Bogart's Shrimp Pasta with Sun-Dried Tomatoes, 108
Butterflake Rolls, 33
Butterfly Shrimp with Bacon, 51

C

Chart House Fried Rice, 87
Chess Pie, 136
Chicken and Pumpkin Laulau, 114
Chicken Estufao, 7
Chicken Kelaguen, 59
Chinese Tea Cookies, 157
Coconut Candy, 137
Coconut Cream Pie, 139
Cola Cake, 5
Cold Oven Pound Cake, 149
Cornish Hen Pot Roast, 111
Crêpes, 23
Crock Pot Lasagna, 11
Crouching Lion Slavonic Steak, 126

D

Don Ho's Kālua Quesadilla, 43

F

Fresh Apple Spice Cake, 131
Frosted Flake Chocolate Chip Cookies, 143

G

Gai See Mein, 93
Golden Dragon Mongolian Lamb, 117
Golden Dragon Pork Char Siu, 35
Green Goddess Dressing, 75
Green Tea Mousse, 144
Grilled Steak Salad, 14
Guamanian Red Rice, 95

» Recipe Index

H

Haleiwa Joe's Seafood Grill, 46
Halekulani Cranberry Sauce, 73
Hari Kojima's King Crab Dip, 77
Harry's Famous Rum Cake, 153
Hasu Sanbaizuke, 67
Herb's Scout Stew, 105
House Without a Key Tarragon Vinaigrette, 84

I

Ilikai Hoisin Vinaigrette, 79
Inari Tuna-Tofu, 68
India House Chicken Curry, 112
Island-Style Custard Pie, 140

J

Japanese Christmas Cake, 159
Jean's Bakery Danish Tea Cake, 29
Junkyard Chili, 3
Just Like Mom's Pork Tofu, 122

K

Kahala Moon Banana Mac-Nut Praline Tart, 134
Kahala Moon Fire-Roasted Portobello with Balsamic Roasted Garlic Jus, 49
Kaka'ako Kitchen Balsamic Vinaigrette, 78
Kaka'ako Kitchen Basil-Bleu Cheese Dressing, 78
Kaka'ako Kitchen Banana-Poi Bread, 17
Kona Brewing Co. Strawberry Spinach Salad, 65

L

L&L Drive-Inn Barbecued Chicken, 113
Lemon Tofu Pie, 160
Liberty House Garden Court Biscuits, 19
Little Chicken Biscuits, 37
Long Rice Special, 96
Lunalilo School Spaghetti, 103
L'Uraku Crunchy Shrimp with Tomato Lomi, 39

M

Macadamia Nut Shortbread, 155
Magic Macaroni and Cheese, 13
Mariposa Papaya-Champagne Vinaigrette, 82
Mediterraneo Salad, 61
Melt-in-Your-Mouth Macadamia Shortbread, 155
Microwave Rice, 98
Miniature Taro Cheesecake, 156
Mom's Chinese-Syle Steamed Fish, 15
Moon Cakes, 146

N

New Red Velvet Cake, 150
Ninniku-ya 'Ahi Mascarpone, 41

O

Oahu Country Club Bread Pudding, 21
Oka with Crabmeat, 81
Orchids Scalloped Potato Gratin, 64

Recipe Index   163

P

Palm Terrace Curried Chicken Salad with Papaya, 58
Palomino Chop Chop Salad, 63
Palomino Euro Bistro Paella, 119
Paul Chun's Pancakes, 27
Pickled Radish, 67
Pig's Feet Soup, 121
Pineapple Nut Bread, 30
Plumeria Beach House Salad Niçoise, 57
Popcorn Shrimp with Bloody Mary Aioli, 47
Portuguese Milk Bread (Pao de Leite), 25
Prince Court Baked Oysters with Escargot, 50
Punahou Mango Chutney, 80

R

Rainbow Drive-In Shoyu Chicken, 123
Red Sauce, 71
Rice for a Crowd, 97
Ryan's Grill Cajun Chicken Fettuccini, 124

S

Sam Choy's Tripe Poke, 53
Sansei Umeboshi Dressing, 85
Seafood Laulau, 115
Side Street Inn Garlic Edamame, 38
Slow Cooker Laulau, 116
Spicy Kim Chee Fried Rice, 12
Stir-Fried Saimin, 91

T

Takuwan, 66
Thai Valley Cuisine Green Curry, 127
Toasted Coconut Macaroons, 145

V

Vegetarian Laulau, 115

W

Whole Kumquat Preserves, 83

Y

Yellow Cake, 161
Yellow Sauce, 71

» Recipe Index

Index

A

A Little Bit of Saigon, 128-129
Aaron's Atop the Ala Moana, 72
Angelo Pietro, 54-55, 100-101
apple, 4, 73, 131
apricot preserves, 146
Arora, Ram, 112
avocado, 89

B

Bailey's Irish cream, 132-133
baking soda, 17, 27, 29-30, 44, 83,
    131, 143, 150-151
balsamic vinegar, 49, 57, 60, 63, 78,
    106-107
bamboo shoots, 93, 122, 126
banana, 17, 30, 134-135
base
    chicken base, 103, 105
    beef base, 105
basil leaves, 45, 61, 63, 78
BBQ sauce, 43
bean paste, sweetened , 146
bean sprouts, 14, 91, 93
beans
    kidney beans, 3
    garbanzo beans, 63
    soy beans, 38, 106
beef
    steak, tri-tip, 14
    filet mignon, 46, 126
    ground beef, 3, 103-104
    beef chuck roast, 105
    beef short rib, 104-105
    cross-rib roast, 3
beet, 150-151
bell pepper, 3, 12, 72, 127

Big City Diner, 26
biscuit, 36
Bloody Mary, 46-47
Bogart's, 108
brandy, 35, 117
bread
    bread pudding, 20-21
    bread, french, 49
Bruhl, Bill, 124
buttermilk, 28-29, 47, 136
Byron's Drive Inn, 70

C

Cades, Marsha, 78
cake, 4-5, 18, 26, 28-29, 64, 91, 131,
    146-155, 158-159, 161
cake mix, 4-5, 152-153
candied wintermelon, 36-37
caper, 72
cardamom seeds, 112
carrot, 91, 93
celery, 2, 58, 76-77, 91, 93, 105
Chaowasaree, Chai, 14
char siu, 34-35, 87, 91
Chart House, 87
cheese
    cream cheese, 40, 64, 76-77, 132-
        133, 150-151, 156
    cottage cheese, 10-11, 13
    mozzarella, 11, 43
    Parmesan, 11, 63-64 108, 124
    provolone cheese, 63
    cheddar cheese, 13, 43
    gorgonzola, 65
    bleu cheese, 78
    American cheese, 102-103
cherries, dried, 150
Chiang, Steve, 34, 117

chicken
  chicken thighs, 7-8, 113-114, 118, 123
  cornish game hen, 110-111
  chicken tenderloins, 124
  chicken drumsticks, 9
  chicken breasts, 58, 101, 109
chili powder, 3, 112
chocolate chips, 143
chorizo, 118-119
chow mein, 90, 92-93
Choy, Sam, 53
chung choy (pickled turnip), 15
cider vinegar, 80
citron, 80
clam juice, 118
Coca-Cola, 109
cocoa powder, 5, 150-151
coconut
  coconut juice, 59, 129
  coconut milk, 81, 114, 127-128
coffee, 4, 16, 132, 150
cookie crumbs, 156
corn, 6, 12, 39, 83, 105, 137
Cornflakes, 163
cranberries, 73
cream of mushroom soup, 76-77
cream of tartar, 158-159
Crouching Lion, 126
cucumber, 14, 66, 89, 128
cumin, 3, 119, 125
curry paste, 127
curry powder, 58

D

daikon, 55, 66, 121
dark beer, 45
dates, 146
DeAngelo, Fred, 62, 118
dehydrated onions, 103
Denis, Robert, 126

Don Ho's Island Grill, 43
Drager, Milan, 56
dressing, 14, 55, 60-63, 66, 69, 72-75, 78, 82, 84-85, 100
dry mustard, 13, 74, 85
duck bone, 92
duck egg yolk, 146

E

eggplant, 127
Endo, Eiyuki, 40
escargot, 50

F

Fitzek, Mark, 46
fish sauce, 7, 14, 39, 127, 129
fish
  'ahi, 40-41, 52, 56-57, 70, 81
  anchovy, 45, 74-75
  mahimahi, 118
  tuna, 56, 68
  snapper, 81
  mullet, 15
  kumu, 15
flour
  quinoa flour, 150-151
  whole-wheat flour, 150-151
  cake flour, 29, 154-155, 158-159
  sifted flour, 131, 134, 159, 161
food coloring, 35, 66-67, 75, 137, 156
Franks, Dennis, 26
French bread, 49
Frosted Flakes, 143
frosting, 5, 150-151

G

Garden Court restaurant, 18
garlic paste, 49
gelatin, 76-77, 120, 139, 160
ginger, 2, 15, 42-43, 67, 73, 79-80,

83, 91, 96, 105, 109, 112-113, 117, 121-123
Golden Dragon restaurant, 35, 116-117
graham cracker, 156
gravy, 54, 92-93, 110
green tea, 144

H

Haleiwa Joe's, 46
Halekulani, 64, 73
ham, 12, 23, 91-93, 96
Hawaiian chili peppers, 53
Hawaiian salt, 50, 105, 114-116, 121
heavy cream, 21, 64, 144
hoisin sauce, 35, 79, 117
hondashi, 85, 100-101
honey, 18, 26, 78, 106-107, 157
Honpa Hongwanji Hawai'i Betsuin, 66, 83, 104
hot pepper sauce, 38
House Without a Key, 84

I

iceberg lettuce, 55, 85
inarizushi (cone sushi) wrapper, 68
India House, 112
instant pudding, 152-153
Italian sausage, 11

J

jalapeno pepper, 3
Jean's Bakery & Fountain, 28
jus, 49

K

kabocha, 56-57
Kahala Moon, 48-49
Kaka'ako Kitchen, 17, 78

kalamata olives, 57
ketchup, 35, 45, 51, 71
kim chee, 12, 52, 66, 87
kochujang, 52-53
Kojima, Hari, 77
Kona Brewing Co., 65
kumquat, 83

L

L&L Drive-Inn, 112-113
L'Uraku, 39
lamb, 40, 106-107, 117
Le Bistro,, 106
lettuce, iceberg , 55, 85
liqueur, 132-133
lotus root, 66-67
luncheon meat, 96

M

macadamia nuts, 29, 65, 135, 154-155
maltose, 36-37
mango, 14, 30, 58, 80
Manuel, Randy, 87
maple syrup, 29
marinade, 2, 7-9, 15, 34-35, 78, 106-107, 109, 113, 117, 125, 128-129
Mariposa, 82
Mediterraneo, 60-61
Masutani, Shane, 109
mayonnaise, 45-47, 58, 71, 75-78, 84, 88
Mendiola-Flores, Celeste, 20
meringue, 138-139, 144-145
Morales, Hector, 58
mushroom
    shiitake mushrooms, 68, 88, 91, 93, 96, 100, 121
    portobello mushroom, 48-49
mustard cabbage, pickled (sin choy), 2
mustard, dry, 13, 74, 85

Index « 167

N

nam yue (red fermented bean curd), 37
Ninniku-ya, 40-41
Nishida, Colin, 38
nishimi kubu, 121
noodles
    lasagna, whole wheat, 11
    penne rigatoni, 108
    spaghetti, 100-104
    fettuccini, 124
    macaroni, whole wheat, 13
    chow mein noodles, 90, 93
    saimin, 90-91

O

Oahu Country Club, 20-21
oatmeal, 17, 26, 135
olive oil, 38-39, 41, 49, 57, 60-61, 63,
    72, 74, 78, 82, 89, 107-108, 111,
    118, 126
olive, kalamata, 57
onion, 2, 7, 9, 11-12, 14-15, 39, 41,
    44-45, 53, 59, 65, 68, 71, 74-75, 77,
    79, 82, 84-85, 87, 91, 93, 95-96,
    114-115, 117-118, 122, 124-125, 128
onions, dehydrated, 103
orange, 73, 79-80, 89, 94, 134-135
orange juice, 79, 135
Orchids, 64

P

Palm Terrace, 58
Palomino, 62-63, 118
papaya, 58, 82, 89
pear, 73
peas, 51, 89, 118-119
pesto, 108
pie crust, 132-133, 160
pie shell, 136, 139-141
pig's feet, 120-121
pimentos, 95

pineapple, 30, 134-135, 160
pineapple juice, 135
plum sauce, 79
Plumeria Beach House, 56-57
poi, 17, 74, 156
pork
    kālua pork, 42-43
    pork butt, 35
    portuguese sausage, 3, 104-105
potato, 24-25, 39, 55, 64, 114-115
potato salad, 55
potato starch, 39
powdered milk, 146-147
Prince Court, 50
pudding, instant, 152-153
pumpkin, 56, 114, 138

R

radish, 55, 66-67
Rainbow Drive-In, 123
raisins, 21, 26, 58, 80, 131, 146
red wine, 2, 15, 60-61, 72, 74, 106-
    107, 110
relish, 71
Renaissance Ilikai Hotel, 79
rice, 7, 12, 51, 54, 66-68, 79, 82, 85-
    90, 94-99, 118-119, 122
rice vinegar, 7, 51, 66-67, 79, 82, 85, 89
Ro, Kelvin, 48, 134
romaine hearts, 63
rum, 152-153
Ryan's Grill, 124

S

saimin, 90-91
sake, 66-67, 79, 82, 110, 121, 150
salad, 14, 39, 55-63, 65-66, 69-70,
    72, 74-75, 78-79, 82, 84-85, 96,
    99-100
salami, 63
Sansei Seafood Restaurant & Sushi
    Bar, 85

seafood
  shrimp, 31, 39, 46-47, 51, 59, 68, 92, 108, 114-115, 118-119, 127
  oyster, 2, 12, 50, 87, 90, 93
  calamari, 115
  scallops, 115
  clam, 70, 100, 118
  mussels, 81, 118-119
  crab, 59, 76-77, 118-119
  See also Fish
seasoning, 44, 61, 69, 88-91, 95, 100-101
Side Street Inn, 38
sour cream, 6, 17, 43, 45, 75, 133
spaghetti sauce mix, 103
sparkling wine, 82
spice blend, 124-125
spinach, 10-11, 22, 65, 101, 108
Sprite, 4, 109
stock
  chicken stock, 49, 117, 119, 124
  fish stock, 100-101, 118
  veal stock, 107
strawberries, 23, 65, 159
string beans, 93
sugar
  Chinese brown sugar (wong tong), 157
  powdered sugar, 5, 29, 134, 139, 145, 148, 150, 159
sun-dried tomato, 47
sweet potato, 114-115
sweet vinegar sauce, 67
sweetened bean paste, 146

T

tarragon, 75, 84
Thai chili-garlic sauce, 12
Thai Valley Cuisine, 127
Thirakoun, Carole, 127
tofu, 35, 68, 115, 122, 160
tomato, 3, 11, 39, 47, 57, 62-63, 72, 89, 103, 105, 108, 124-125
tomato paste, 11, 105
tomato sauce, 3, 11, 103, 105, 124-125
tomato, sun-dried, 47
tripe, 52-53
turkey breast , 63, 109
turkey, ground, 10-11
turmeric, 112

U

ume, 55, 85

V

vermouth, 110-111, 119
vinaigrette, 39, 57, 62, 65, 72, 74, 78-79, 82, 84

W

walnuts, 30, 131, 153
wet bean curd, 35
whipping cream, 41, 139, 159
whisky, 2
white wine, 65, 75, 100, 110-111, 118
wine vinegar
  red wine vinegar, 60-61, 72, 74
  white wine vinegar, 65
wintermelon, candied, 36-37
wong tong (Chinese brown sugar), 157
Worcestershire sauce, 38, 50, 103, 123-124

Y

yeast, 24-25, 32-33

Z

zucchini, 2, 10-11

Index 169

About the Author

Betty Shimabukuro is a managing editor at the *Honolulu Star-Advertiser* and writer of the column "By Request" in the paper's weekly Food section. She came upon the challenge of hunting recipes in 1998 for the *Honolulu Star-Bulletin*, after many years of news writing and editing. Her cooking training at the time involved nothing more than a spotty apprenticeship with her mother, Betty Zane Shimabukuro, a legendary home economist with the University of Hawai'i's Cooperative Extension Service, but she has since been learning from some of Hawai'i's best chefs and home cooks.

Shimabukuro is a graduate of the UH journalism program and Kaiser High School (Go, Cougars!). Her desire to work in daily newspapers took her first to Guam, then across the country to Florida, then back again to California. She met her husband, Rob Perez, at her first newspaper job at the *Pacific Daily News* on Guam, and today they have three children—Justin, Christine and Caleb—who have been variously amused and distressed by the experimental dinners that are part of a food writer's home life.